OLD MOORE'S

HOROSCOPE AND ASTRAL DIARY

•

LIBRA

foulsham

LONDON • NEW YORK • TORONTO • SYDNEY

foulsham
Yeovil Road, Slough, Berkshire, SL1 4JH

ISBN 0-572-01911-4

Printed in: Great Britain at
Cox & Wyman Ltd, Reading

CONTENTS

OLD MOORE'S HOROSCOPE AND ASTRAL DIARY

Old Moore's Horoscope and Astral Diary represents a major departure from the usual format of publications dedicated to popular Sun-sign astrology. In this book, more attention than ever before has been focused on the discovery of the 'real you', through a wealth of astrological information, presented in an easy to follow and interesting form, and designed to provide a comprehensive insight into your fundamental nature.

The interplay of the Sun and Moon form complex cycles that are brought to bear on each of us in different ways. In the pages that follow I will explain how a knowledge of these patterns in your life can make relationships with others easier and general success more possible. Realising when your mind and body are at their most active or inactive, and at what times your greatest efforts are liable to see you winning through, can be of tremendous importance. In addition, your interaction with other zodiac types is explored, together with a comprehensive explanation of your Sun-sign nature,

In the Astral Diary you will discover a day-to-day reading covering a fifteen-month period. The readings are compiled from solar, lunar and planetary relationships as they bear upon your own zodiac sign. In addition, easy-to-follow graphic charts offer you at a glance an understanding of the way that your personal life-cycles are running; what days are best for maximum effort and when your system is likely to be regenerating.

Because some people want to look deeper into the fascinating world of personal astrology, there is a section of the book allowing a more in-depth appraisal of the all-important zodiac sign that was 'Rising' at the time of your birth. You can also look at your own personal 'Moon Sign' using simple to follow instructions to locate the position of this very significant heavenly body on the day that you were born.

From a simple-to-follow diary section, on to an intimate understanding of the ever-changing child of the solar system that you are, my Horoscope and Astral Diary will allow you to unlock potential that you never even suspected you had.

With the help and guidance of the following pages, Old Moore wishes you a happy and prosperous future.

HERE'S LOOKING AT YOU

A ZODIAC PORTRAIT OF LIBRA
(24th SEPTEMBER - 23rd OCTOBER)

Often thought of as being the best-looking sign of the zodiac, it is true to say that your ruling planet Venus endows you not only with social graces, charm and beautiful manners, but corresponding physical beauty too. The symbol for Libra depicts a pair of Scales, a balance which suggests a sort of symmetry and evenness. Indeed, this is invariably reflected in the Libran face. Librans usually look good from any angle, and are well aware of the fact, probably spending more hours in front of the mirror than any of their zodiac cousins.

The hair is abundant and silky, and the skin of excellent quality. Features often include an aquiline nose and a delicate chin. Libran eyes are attractive and have a soothing quality, tending more towards darker rather than lighter shades. There is always a twinkle there too, both playful and seductive. In terms of dress, nobody can compare with Librans of either gender. Styles chosen are tasteful, with a good sense of coordination and actual colour, courtesy of their ruling planet Venus. Odd styles and colours are combined, but they invariably come together wonderfully and enhance the fineness of the Libran physique. As to the kind of clothes peg a Libran might make, much depends on the diet, since Libra is one of the zodiac signs that is inclined to put on weight if a healthy diet is not maintained. Libra more than any other sign needs to be particularly aware of its food intake. The kidneys, that complex internal regulating system, are ruled by this sign. Upsets to the general peace of mind of Libra are often reflected psychosmatically in kidney ailments.

Despite your penchant for a well balanced mind-body relationship, you are prone to excesses. Your ruler, Venus, is a planet of pleasure and you can be particularly sensitive to inner disorders, often borne of a distinct lack of dietry fibre.

THE INTENTION

What could it be that really motivates the courteous, diplomatic, socially polished people born under this sign. The answer is 'relationship'. This is to say, the way in which one person, idea or object is contrasted with another. In terms of relationships, this involves an act of comparison and Libra is motivated by the need to seek out the perfect compliment to itself, which naturally entails looking for a person who can fulfil this role.

Looking at the symbol for this sign, the Scales, we recognise a device utilised to balance out weights equally on both sides. This tells a great deal about what drives Libra forward in life. The Libran is always looking for the happy medium, and as many ways as possible to offset the natural inbalances that it comes across in life as a whole. Indeed for some this becomes a life's mission, and some can become quite unhappy simply because life isn't always fair or even handed.

The ruling planet of Venus, fills Libra with a love of true values; of beauty that can be considered attractive to the eye. Libra will seek to make its world as pleasurable and harmonious as possible. Those born under the Scales will also seek to engender the same neatness and order in their relationships. Intense and dramatic ties are not likely to be cultivated and Librans may sometimes be accused of preferring superficiality.

YOUR VIRTUES

Librans are a positive delight to be with, and those who are possessed of Libran friends or lovers, wives or husbands, know only too well how true this is. Possessing all the social graces, your finely tuned sensitivities allow you to home in on the other person, making him or her feel instantly at ease.

All Air signs have an easy-going manner, Libra more than most and people born under the Scales can be relied upon to be courteous, polite and warm. You tend to place great emphasis on the conventions of social interaction; etiquette, good manners etc., and can be relied upon to act properly in almost any given situation. Accommodating, engaging friendliness is the hallmark of this sign, partly because you find it so easy to relate to other people. Even the most potentially destructive or

7

difficult situations can be dealt with by someone of your sign, so it should not be surprising to learn that many of the world's greatest diplomats were born with their Sun in Libra.

The pitfalls of a Libran in marriage will be dealt with presently, though for the moment it is important to realise that the very affability of this sign, together with the natural good looks almost endemic here, means that Librans rarely go short of company, particularly in a romantic sense. You know how to treat your partner, and especially how to flatter them. In this situation, as in most others, you display charm, poise, intelligence and spontaneity. In fact your attitudes towards those close to you do not differ markedly from those displayed to the world at large.

YOUR VICES

Not a particularly easy section to deal with this, because in the main 'vices' would tend to alude to those qualities of nature over which the recipient has some control, together with an understanding of some definite 'errant' behaviour. In the case of Libra however, many of the apparent faults are nothing more than extensions of virtues. Alas, no one is beyond criticism, not even you, though if you have the typical easily deflated ego that Librans tend to inherit, perhaps you should take the following with a slight pinch of salt.

It is in the sphere of relationships that problems often occur because, to be quite frank, you don't really know how to remain faithful in thought, word and deed. The last thing that you intend to do is to upset anyone, but you are so popular that you can't help attracting attention, and nor is your ego strong enough to shun the compliments that come your way. Add to this a slight tendency towards being weak-willed and you have the perfect recipe for infidelity. Quite often you can be accused of being superficial, a criticism that tends to be levelled at many Air sign individuals. In reality you are simply interested in everything, so that in the end there is never enough time to concentrate on specifics, even when these are obviously of supreme importance to others.

Decisions are not easy for you to make, leading to the adage often cited for Libra, 'I used to be uncertain but now I'm not sure'. In fact this is a slight misunderstanding of the facts because those born under the Scales often do know what they want, but need to weigh up all options so carefully that others may tire of waiting so long before a decision is actually made. At your worst you can charge through the feelings and emotions of others like a bull elephant, not realising that you have done any damage at all. This especially is bound to surprise you because you would not consider yourself to be in the least selfish. How could you be? After all you're perfect!

LIVING A HAPPY LIFE

You need a neat and happy environment to live in if you are to be contented with your lot. Like all Air sign individuals, you also revel in good company, together with a job that allows your flair and individuality to show. You would not consider yourself to be a particularly complicated person and can gain greatly by keeping your day-to-day life as simple as possible. The same could be said to be the case with your diet, and the healthiest Librans tend to be 'light snackers' rather than regular imbibers of rich, heavy meals.

Concentrating on details is not especially easy for you, since your natural desire is for superficiality. Nevertheless, where relationships especially are concerned, a deeper thinking Libran does need to be nurtured if true happiness is to be found. Since this runs against the natural tendencies of your sign, there is no wonder that yours is the sign of the zodiac that is most likely to suffer marital problems.

In work, you function best when your communicational and diplomatic skills can find room. Dirty or heavy, manual work is less likely to interest you. Many Librans are very creative, and this is another fact to bear in mind before you decide exactly what career is likely to suit you the best. It is not unusual for those born under the Scales, or any Air sign for that matter, to opt for self-employment, though the Libran may be beter at actually getting down to the more glamerous parts of the job in hand, preferring to leave the tedious or less interesting tasks to other people if at all possible.

By far and away the most important fact for Librans, when it comes to living a happy life, is the creation of the sort of environment that allows scope for the full use of the many and varied skills given to the sign at birth. People in your vicinity play an important part in the scenario, because you hate vulgar or insensitive types.

WHAT'S RISING

YOUR RISING SIGN AND PERSONALITY

Perhaps you have come across this term 'Rising Sign' when looking at other books on astrology and may have been somewhat puzzled as to what it actually means. To those not accustomed to astrological jargon it could sound somewhat technical and mysterious, though in fact, in terms of your own personal birth chart, it couldn't be simpler. The Rising Sign is simply that part of the zodiac occupying the eastern horizon at the time of your birth. Because it is a little more difficult to discover than your sun-sign, many writers of popular astrology have tended to ignore it, which is a great shame, because, together with the Sun, your Rising Sign is the single most important factor in terms of setting your personality. So much so, that no appraisal of your astrological nature could be complete without it.

Your Rising Sign, also known as your 'Ascendant' or 'Ascending Sign' plays a great part in your looks - yes, astrology can even predict what you are going to be like physically. In fact, this is a very interesting point, because there appears to be a tie-in between astrology and genetics. Professional Astrologers for centuries have noted the close relationship that often exists between the astrological birth chart of parents and those of their offspring, so that, if you look like your Mother or Father, chances are that there is a close astrological tie-up. Rising signs especially appear to be handed down through families.

The first impression that you get, in an astrological sense, upon meeting a stranger, is not related to their sun-sign but to the zodiac sign that was rising at the moment they came into the world. The Rising Sign is particularly important because it modifies the way that you display your Sun-sign to the world at large. A good example of this might be that of Britain's best-known ex- Prime minister, Margaret Thatcher. This dynamic and powerful lady is a Libran by Sun-sign placing, indicating a light-hearted nature, pleasure loving and very flexible. However, Mrs Thatcher has Scorpio as her Rising Sign, bringing a steely determination and a tremendous capacity for work. It also bestows an iron will and the power to thrive under pressure.

Here lies the true importance of the Rising Sign, for Mr Thatcher almost certainly knows a woman who most other people do not. The Rising Sign is a protective shell, and not until we know someone quite well do we start to discover the Sun-sign nature that hides within this often tough outer coat of astrological making. Your Rising Sign also represents your basic self-image, the social mask that is often so useful; and even if you don't think that you conform to the interpretation of your Ascendant, chances are that other people will think that you do.

The way that an individual looks, walks, sits and generally presents themselves to the world is all down to the Rising Sign. For example, a person possessed of Gemini Rising is apt to be very quick, energetic in all movements, deliberate in mannerisms and with a cheerful disposition. A bearer of a Taurean Ascendant on the other hand would probably not be so tall, more solid generally, quieter in aspect and calmer in movement. Once you come to understand the basics of astrology it is really very easy to pick out the Rising Signs of people that you come across, even though the Sun-sign is often more difficult to pin down. Keep an eye open for the dynamic and positive Aries Rising individual, or the retiring, shy but absolutely magnetic quality of of the Piscean Ascendant. Of course, in astrology, nothing is quite that simple. The position of a vast array of heavenly bodies at the time of birth also has to be taken into account, particularly that of the Moon and the inner planets Mercury and Venus. Nevertheless a knowledge of your Rising sign can be an invaluable aid in getting to know what really makes you tick as an individual.

To ascertain the exact degree of your Rising sign takes a little experience and recourse to some special material. However, I have evolved a series of tables that will enable you to discover at a glance what your Rising Sign is likely to be. All you need to know is the approximate time of your birth. At the back of the book you will find the necessary table related to your Sun-sign. Simply look down the left-hand column until you find your approximate time of birth, am or pm. Now scan across the top of the table to the place where your date of birth is shown. Look for the square where the two pieces of information connect and there is your Rising Sign. Now that you know what your Rising Sign is, read on, and learn even more about the fascinating interplay of astrological relationship.

LIBRA WITH LIBRA RISING

A double helping of Libra means that you must have been born around dawn, and ensures that in your approach to the world at large, you typify all aspects, both good and not so good, of the sign of the scales. This indicates that you are courteous and affable, fun to be around, and are able to make a great impression on others. Popularity is unlikely to be in doubt in the case of this combination because it is easy for you to make others feel at ease in your company, not to mention being able to sort out all their little problems too.

You are life's born diplomat and should hold down a job that allows you to use this skill to the full. In a more negative sense, it is true that you will find it almost impossible to be decisive and will be inclined to hedge your bets under most circumstances. Relationships of the personal sort can be something of a problem to you because you find it somewhat dificult to give yourself exclusively to one person. Continuity is what you lack, and is what you must seek to put into your life by continued effort. Something that you will never be short of is company.

LIBRA WITH SCORPIO RISING

Perhaps it's the air of subtle mystery, or the cool and distant charisma that makes you so very attractive. A combination of the softness, charm and affability of Libra and the more sultry, dark magic of the Scorpion, create an infusion that few could resist.

There is a powerful, almost brooding aura here, which others could see as somehow threatening on occasions, but which enhances the natural magnetism of Scorpio all the same. Although the Libran side of you is quite sociable, still you would benefit from shutting yourself away from the world from time to time, in order to get in touch with your deeper self. To this end you could derive a great deal of good through meditaion, which also allows you to sort out some of the more complicated thoughts that bounce around your brain from morning until night. You are psychic to quite a high degree, though you could be too fatalistic for your own and other people's good. On the whole, you probably display more of the qualities of Scorpio than you do of Libra.

LIBRA WITH SAGITTARIUS RISING

With your charming and winning ways, it is no wonder that you are high in the popularity stakes; at best you can be described as vivacious and attractive, at worst superficial and trivial. This stems from your need to present an attractive and appealing front to the world and to show yourself as one who is capable of placating others. You simply must be accepted as part of the group, and this fact predominates through almost every facet of your life. In some ways you lack a personal sense of identity, even though others tell you that you are smart, talented, attractive and loveable. Perhaps you should believe them more because what they are saying is very likely to be true.

Personality-wise, you are outgoing, living for the world of social interaction, friends and acquaintances. Your easy-going nature wins others round and you cannot bear unpleasantness of any sort. Sagittarius Rising tends to add zest to some of the slightly quieter qualities of Libra but everything must be tempered to the conventions of social politeness, good manners and etiquette. You can be a terrible flirt and relationships are a problem long-term for some people with this combination.

LIBRA WITH CAPRICORN RISING

As both Capricorn and Libra are Cardinal signs, you possess great initiative and the ability to set things into motion. Organising people is your main forte, and you carry it out in the gentle and diplomatic manner that so typifies the sign of the Scales. You need to be involved in what is going on in the world and would be good in the spheres of public relations, enterprise or politics.

Behind this facade and invisible to most people, is a much more private sort of individual, and one that proves to be a sentimentalist with a strong attachment to the past and an emotional vulnerability. You manage to retain an attractive appearance that could well be quite ageless, which is probably a good thing since you place great emphasis on the way that you appear when viewed by others. Avoid a devious streak and stick with the truth on all occasions. Relationships can be every bit as difficult for you as they are apt to be with any Libran contact, perhaps ever more so in your case.

LIBRA WITH AQUARIUS RISING

The world sees you as a warm and caring human being, and that wouldn't be so far from the truth. However, beneath that apparently sincere and companionable exterior, you may not be quite as you appear at first sight. Libra and Aquarius are both Air signs and as such can be rather cool when it comes to formulating more intimate relationships. This can make you rather difficult to get to know on a deeply personal level. Any social encounter is grist to the mill as far as you are concerned and you have no difficulty at all in forging a successful career for yourself since you are very capable. Most of the time you live for, and in, a world of pleasure and romance; charming to behold and fun to be with.

Behind closed doors you are a different kettle of fish however, that is if anyone could ever persuade you to stop more than five minutes in the same place. Personal relationships can be a real problem; you want to be faithful and loving, but there are a world of possibilities out there, and everyone loves you so much. Would it be fair to tie yourself down to just one?

LIBRA WITH PISCES RISING

You are always careful about your own appearance and could come across to the world as a seeker of personal perfection. Beauty in all its forms is important to you, though never more so than when you are looking at yourself.

Your nature is flirtatious and you know how to make people like you, which could be of great importance since you would run a mile sooner than admit you had an enemy. The more earthy aspects of humanity are something that you fail to recognise at all, or if they are forced upon you are likely to be put to the back of your mind. This is the ostrich within you.

Showing a tendency to compromise, even regarding issues that might be of some importance to you, you seek to ford the stream of life making as few ripples as possible on the way. More assertiveness would work wonders, especially in matters related to your career, since you often find yourself standing at the back of the queue, even when you have more than enough about you to push your way to the front. As with all signs trying to relate to Libra, there are certain to be contradictions he within this combination.

LIBRA WITH ARIES RISING

Libra does bring a gentler aspect to bear on the generally volatile Aries component of your nature and makes for a far more complex character than would be expected from either sign alone. All the same, you can be fairly short-tempered and will not suffer fools gladly. You are quite prepared to take the initiative in social encounters, when beginning new projects or laying down plans generally. On occasions you manage to score your points by being unobtrusive, so there can be a few contradictions thrown up by this combination.

Perhaps your best talent lies in your ability to make others feel that they are very important, which means that they will do almost anything for you in return. This makes you socially popular and assures you of avid support. Unlike Aries, you have as much interest in the world at large as you do with regard to your own ideas and efforts. This makes you appear to be distinctly unselfish when viewed through the eyes of other people, yet another reason for the singular popularity that you can enjoy.

LIBRA WITH TAURUS RISING

Libra sits comfortably with almost any sign, though few more harmoniously than that of Taurus. You graduated from the charm school of life at a very early age, carrying first class honours and a degree in coercion. With the most subtle of persuasion you manage to acquire all the things that the Taurean within you desires and can actually find other people grateful that they have had the chance to assist you on your way. You are a natural diplomat and peace-maker, filled with Venusian charm and perhaps also possessed of the stunning good looks that are often to be found with this combination. Aware of the attractive picture you present, you may well go out of your way to complete the portrait by dressing impeccably and developing a slight obsession with personal hygiene and good health.

The presence of Libra means that you are not as earthy as the typical Taurean would be, and this indicates that there is significantly more flexibility within your nature. Look for interests that involve you with others. Work in a complaints department and you may even have people apologising to you for having bought your shoddy goods.

LIBRA WITH GEMINI RISING

There is no doubt that you were born under a wandering star, for both Gemini and Libra are 'air signs', increasing the inquisitive qualities of your nature and making it vital for you to be constantly searching for answers to a million questions that beset you. Full of the charm that so typifies the sign of Libra, and which is also to be seen in Gemini when at its best, you are, never the less, something of a social butterfly. You undoubtedly have many cultured friends who enable you to retain your basic assertion that the world is a place of harmony and beauty, and can be disappointed when you realise that often it isn't.

Most Libran Geminis enjoy travelling, are delightful and witty companions and can always be relied upon to spin a good 'yarn' guaranteed to entertain the many and varied ranks of people they meet on their sojourn through life. It is fair to say that you often deal in superficialities, don't really like to get your hands dirty, except in the garden, and prefer the company of people who share your unique and peaceful view of the world.

LIBRA WITH CANCER RISING

Others may be forgiven for being led to believe that here is a person who will go to the ends of the earth to be generous, helpful or self-sacrificing; submissively adapting to the whiles and whims of others, while personal desires and ambitions take a back seat. Although this description applies well in some cases, it is possible that your apparent submission to others disguises an ulterior motive residing beneath the surface. There is no sinister element to your personality, it is merely you know what you want and how to get it. With this useful combination you attain your desires by the appropriate amount of charm, coercion, generosity and if need be adaptation. Both Cancer and Libra are cardinal signs and this brings initiative, action and go-getting. Your ability for communicating with others has a disarming quality and you can make them fall under your spell without them even realising.

Libra allows you to be at your best in all possible situations. In the end though, it is only those closest to you who recognise the depth of your being.

LIBRA WITH LEO RISING

The combination of Fire and Air evident in this matching of Sun and Rising sign can make for a very comfortable and rewarding combination. It is true that some people may find you to be just a touch fickle and this might make them somewhat reticent to be totally honest with you. You may also find it less than easy to take other people's feelings seriously, though in the main you focus on the lighter side of life, being refreshing to know and happy to be the sort of person that the zodiac has made you. Originality is the key as far as your nature is concerned and you take delight in anything that is out of the ordinary.

One of your most noticeable traits is the need you have of other people. Both Leo and Libra are very sociable signs and love the interplay that comes from groups or associations. You need colour, verve and excitement in your life in order to stay happy, though because Libra is ruled by Venus, you also require a certain degree of harmony and the beauty that you can bring to your surroundings. In company you are polite and courteous, you win arguments with a mixture of determination and diplomacy.

LIBRA WITH VIRGO RISING

Hardly the typical Virgo subject, you are much more likely to exude the qualities of your Sun sign Libra. This is a happy combination, for whilst Virgo is inclined to take itself a little too seriously on occasions, Libra is fun loving, easy going, extravagant and certainly more socially oriented than Virgo. With your disarming charm (and probably more than your fair share of good looks) you approach the world with great sensitivity to the needs of others and often put them before yourself.

In many respects, your sense of identity comes from others, and you are very susceptible to what your friends and relatives have to say. In some ways this is an admirable thing, though you should also take time out for self-study, and for coming to terms with your own deeper self. There is an inherent confusion about socialising because Libra always wants to be with others, whilst Virgo is often happy to be alone. In addition, you tend to attract some rather strange types, whose assertiveness can sometimes upset your natural balance.

LIBRA
IN LOVE AND FRIENDSHIP

WANT TO KNOW HOW WELL YOU GET ON WITH OTHER ZODIAC SIGNS?

THE TABLES BELOW DEAL WITH LOVE AND FRIENDSHIP

THE MORE HEARTS THERE ARE AGAINST ANY SIGN OF THE ZODIAC, THE BETTER THE CHANCE OF CUPID'S DART SCORING A DIRECT HIT.

THE SMILES OF FRIENDSHIP DISPLAY HOW WELL YOU WORK OR ASSOCIATE WITH ALL THE OTHER SIGNS OF THE ZODIAC.

Sign	Love (hearts)	Friendship (smiles)
ARIES	♥♥	☺☺
TAURUS	♥♥♥	☺☺
GEMINI	♥♥♥♥♥	☺☺☺☺☺
CANCER	♥♥	☺☺☺
LEO	♥♥♥	☺☺☺
VIRGO	♥♥	☺☺
LIBRA	♥♥♥♥♥	☺☺☺☺
SCORPIO	♥♥♥♥	☺☺☺☺
SAGITTARIUS	♥♥♥	☺☺☺
CAPRICORN	♥	☺☺
AQUARIUS	♥♥♥♥♥	☺☺☺☺☺
PISCES	♥♥♥♥	☺☺☺

THE MOON AND YOUR DAY-TO-DAY LIFE

Look up at the sky on cloudless nights and you are almost certain to see the Earth's closest neighbour in space, engaged in her intricate and complicated relationship with the planet upon which we live. The Moon isn't very large, in fact only a small fraction of the size of the Earth, but it is very close to us in spatial terms, and here lies the reason why the Moon probably has more of a part to play in your day-to-day life than any other body in space.

It is fair to say in astrological terms that if the Sun and Planets represent the hour and minute hands regulating your character swings and mood changes, the Moon is a rapidly sweeping second hand, governing emotions especially, but touching practically every aspect of your life.

Although the Moon moves so quickly, and maintains a staggeringly complex orbital relationship with the Earth, no book charting the possible ups and downs of your daily life could be complete without some reference to lunar action. For this reason I have included a number of the more important lunar cycles that you can observe within your own life, and also give you the opportunity to discover which zodiac sign the Moon occupied when you were born. Follow the instructions below and you will soon have a far better idea of where astrological cycles come from, and the part they play in your life.

SUN MOON CYCLES

The first lunar cycle deals with the relationship that the Moon keeps with your Sun sign. I have made the fluctuations of this pattern easy for you to understand by means of a simple cyclic graph. It appears on the first page of each 'Your Month At A Glance', under the title 'Highs and Lows'. The graph displays the lunar cycle and you will soon learn to understand how its movements have a bearing on your level of energy and your abilities. Once you recognise the patterns, you can work within them, making certain that your maximum efforts are expounded at the most opportune time.

MOON AGE CYCLES

Looking at the second lunar pattern that helps to make you feel the way you do, day-to-day, involves a small amount of work on your part to establish how you slot into the rhythm. However, since Moon Age cycles are one of the most potent astrological forces at work in your life, the effort is more than worthwhile.

This cycle refers to the way that the date of your birth fits into the Moon Phase pattern. Because of the complex relationship of the Earth and the Moon, we see the face of the lunar disc change throughout a period of roughly one month. The time between one New Moon (this is when there is no Moon to be seen) to the next New Moon, is about 29 days. Between the two the Moon would have seemed larger each night until the lunar disc was Full; it would then start to recede back towards New again. We call this cycle the Moon Age Cycle and classify the day of the New Moon as day 0. Full Moon occurs on day 15 with the last day of the cycle being either day 28 or day 29, dependent on the complicated motions of the combined Earth and Moon.

If you know on what Moon Age Day you were born, then you also know how you fit into the cycle. You would monitor the changes of the cycle as more or less tension in your body, an easy or a strained disposition, good or bad temper and so forth. In order to work out your Moon Age Day follow the steps below:

STEP 1: Look at the two New Moon Tables on pages 23 and 24. Down the left hand column you will see every year from 1902 to 1994 listed, and the months of the year appear across the top. Where the year of your birth and the month that you were born coincide, the figure shown indicates the date of the month on which New Moon occurred.

STEP 2: You need to pick the New Moon that occurred prior to your day of birth, so if your birthday falls at the beginning of the month, you may have to refer to the New Moon from the previous month. Once you have established the nearest New Moon prior to your birthday, (and of course in the correct year), all you have to do is count forward to your birthday. (Don't forget that the day of the New Moon is classed as 0.) As an example, if your were born on March 22nd 1962, the last New Moon before your birthday would have occurred on 6th March 1962. Counting forward from 6 to 22 would mean that you were born on Moon Age

Day 16. If your Moon Phase Cycle crosses the end of February, don't forget to check whether or not you were born in a Leap Year. If so you will have to compensate for that fact.

HOW TO USE MOON AGE DAYS

Once you know your Moon Age Day, you can refer to the Diary section of the book, because there, on each day of the year, you will see that the Moon Age Day is listed. The day in each cycle that conforms to your own Moon Age monthly birthday should find you in a positive and optimistic frame of mind Your emotions are likely to be settled and your thinking processes clear and concise. There are other important days that you will want to know about on this cycle, and to make matters simpler I have compiled an easy to follow table on pages 25 and 26. Quite soon you will get to know which Moon Age Days influence you, and how.

Of course Moon Age Cycles, although specific to your own date of birth, also run within the other astrological patterns that you will find described in this book. So, for example, if your Moon Age Day coincided with a particular day of the month, but everything else was working to the contrary, you might be wise to delay any particularly monumental effort until another, more generally favourable, day. Sometimes cycles run together and occasionally they do not; this is the essence of astrological prediction.

YOUR MOON SIGN

Once you have established on what Moon Age Day you were born, it isn't too difficult to also discover what zodiac sign the Moon occupied on the day of your birth. Although the Moon is very small in size compared to some of the solar system's larger bodies, it is very close indeed to the Earth and this seems to give it a special astrological significance. This is why there are many cycles and patterns associated with the Moon that have an important part to play in the lives of every living creature on the face of our planet, Of all the astrological patterns associated with the Moon that have a part to play in your life, none is more potent than those related to the zodiac position of the Moon at birth. Many of the most intimate details of your personal make-up are related to your Moon Sign, and we will look at these now.

HOW TO DISCOVER YOUR MOON SIGN

The Moon moves through each sign of the zodiac in only two to three days. It also has a rather complicated orbital relationship with the Earth; for these reasons it can be difficult to work out what your Zodiac Moon Sign is. However, having discovered your Moon Age Day you are half way towards finding your Moon Sign, and in order to do so, simply follow the steps below:

STEP 1: Make sure that you have a note of your date of birth and also your Moon Age Day.

STEP 2: Look at Zodiac Moon Sign Table 1 on page 27. Find the month of your birth across the top of the table, and your date of birth down the left. Where the two converge you will see a letter. Make a note of the letter that relates to you.

STEP 3: Now turn to Zodiac Moon Sign Table 2 on pages 28 and 30. Look for your Moon Age Day across the top of the tables and the letter that you have just discoverd down the left side. Where the two converge you will see a zodiac sign. The Moon occupied this zodiac sign on the day of your birth.

PLEASE NOTE: The Moon can change signs at any time of the day or night, and the signs listed in this book are generally applicable for 12 noon on each day. If you were born near the start or the end of a particular Zodiac Moon Sign, it is worth reading the character descriptions of adjacent signs. These are listed pages 30to 35. So much of your nature is governed by the Moon at the time of your birth that it should be fairly obvious wich one of the profiles relates to you.

YOUR ZODIAC MOON SIGN EXPLAINED

You will find a profile of all Zodiac Moon Signs on pages 30 to 35, showing in yet another way astrology helps to make you into the individual that you are. In each month in the Astral Diary, in addition to your Moon Age Day, you can also discover your Zodiac Moon Sign birthday (that day when the Moon occupies the same zodiac sign as it did when you were born). At these times you are in the best postion to be emotionally steady and to make the sort of decisions that have real, lasting value.

NEW MOON TABLE

YEAR	JAN	FEB	MAR	APR	MAY	JUN	JUL	AUG	SEP	OCT	NOV	DEC
1902	9	8	9	8	7	6	5	3	2	1/30	29	29
1903	27	26	28	27	26	25	24	22	21	20	19	18
1904	17	15	17	16	15	14	14	12	10	18	8	8
1905	6	5	5	4	3	2	2/31	30	28	28	26	26
1906	24	23	24	23	22	21	20	19	18	17	16	15
1907	14	12	14	12	11	10	9	8	7	6	5	5
1908	3	2	3	2	1/30	29	28	27	25	25	24	24
1909	22	20	21	20	19	17	17	15	14	14	13	12
1910	11	9	11	9	9	7	6	5	3	2	1	1/30
1911	29	28	30	28	28	26	25	24	22	21	20	20
1912	18	17	19	18	17	16	15	13	12	11	9	9
1913	7	6	7	6	5	4	3	2/31	30	29	28	27
1914	25	24	26	24	24	23	22	21	19	19	17	17
1915	15	14	15	13	13	12	11	10	9	8	7	6
1916	5	3	5	3	2	1/30	30	29	27	27	26	25
1917	24	22	23	22	20	19	18	17	15	15	14	13
1918	12	11	12	11	10	8	8	6	4	4	3	2
1919	1/31	-	2/31	30	29	27	27	25	23	23	22	21
1920	21	19	20	18	18	16	15	14	12	12	10	10
1921	9	8	9	8	7	6	5	3	2	1/30	29	29
1922	27	26	28	27	26	25	24	22	21	20	19	18
1923	17	15	17	16	15	14	14	12	10	10	8	8
1924	6	5	5	4	3	2	2/31	30	28	28	26	26
1925	24	23	24	23	22	21	20	19	18	17	16	15
1926	14	12	14	12	11	10	9	8	7	6	5	5
1927	3	2	3	2	1/30	29	28	27	25	25	24	24
1928	21	19	21	20	19	18	17	16	14	14	12	12
1929	11	9	11	9	9	7	6	5	3	2	1	1/30
1930	29	28	30	28	28	26	25	24	22	20	20	19
1931	18	17	19	18	17	16	15	13	12	11	9	9
1932	7	6	7	6	5	4	3	2/31	30	29	2	27
1933	25	24	26	24	24	23	22	21	19	19	17	17
1934	15	14	15	13	13	12	11	10	9	8	7	6
1935	5	3	5	3	2	1/30	30	29	27	27	26	25
1936	24	22	23	21	20	19	18	17	15	15	14	13
1937	12	11	12	12	10	8	8	6	4	4	3	2
1938	1/31	-	2/31	30	29	27	27	25	23	23	22	21
1939	20	19	20	19	19	17	16	15	13	12	11	10
1940	9	8	9	7	7	6	5	4	2	1/30	29	28
1941	27	26	27	26	26	24	24	22	21	20	19	18
1942	16	15	16	15	15	13	13	12	10	10	8	8
1943	6	4	6	4	4	2	2	1/30	29	29	27	27
1944	25	24	24	22	22	20	20	18	17	17	15	15
1945	14	12	14	12	11	10	9	8	6	6	4	4
1946	3	2	3	2	1/30	29	28	26	25	24	23	23
1947	21	19	21	20	19	18	17	16	14	14	12	12

NEW MOON TABLE

YEAR	JAN	FEB	MAR	APR	MAY	JUN	JUL	AUG	SEP	OCT	NOV	DEC
1948	11	9	11	9	9	7	6	5	3	2	1	1/30
1949	29	27	29	28	27	26	25	24	23	21	20	19
1950	18	16	18	17	17	15	15	13	12	11	9	9
1951	7	6	7	6	6	4	4	2	1	1/30	29	28
1952	26	25	25	24	23	22	23	20	29	28	27	27
1953	15	14	15	13	13	11	11	9	8	8	6	6
1954	5	3	5	3	2	1/30	29	28	27	26	25	25
1955	24	22	24	22	21	20	19	17	16	15	14	14
1956	13	11	12	11	10	8	8	6	4	4	2	2
1957	1/30	-	1/31	29	29	27	27	25	23	23	21	21
1958	19	18	20	19	18	17	16	15	13	12	11	10
1959	9	7	9	8	7	6	6	4	3	2/31	30	29
1960	27	26	27	26	26	24	24	22	21	20	19	18
1961	16	15	16	15	14	13	12	11	10	9	8	7
1962	6	5	6	5	4	2	1/31	30	28	28	27	26
1963	25	23	25	23	23	21	20	19	17	17	15	15
1964	14	13	14	12	11	10	9	7	6	5	4	4
1965	3	1	2	1	1/30	29	28	26	25	24	22	22
1966	21	19	21	20	19	18	17	16	14	14	12	12
1967	10	9	10	9	8	7	7	5	4	3	2	1/30
1968	29	28	29	28	27	26	25	24	23	22	21	20
1969	1 9	17	18	16	15	14	13	12	11	10	9	9
1970	7	6	7	6	6	4	4	2	1	1/30	29	28
1971	26	25	26	25	24	22	22	20	19	19	18	17
1972	15	14	15	13	13	11	11	9	8	8	6	6
1973	5	4	5	3	2	1/30	29	28	27	26	25	25
1974	24	22	24	22	21	20	19	17	16	15	14	14
1975	12	11	12	11	11	9	9	7	5	5	3	3
1976	1/31	29	30	29	29	27	27	25	23	23	21	21
1977	19	18	19	18	18	16	16	14	13	12	11	10
1978	9	7	9	7	7	5	5	4	2	2/31	30	29
1979	27	26	27	26	26	24	24	22	21	20	19	18
1980	16	15	16	15	14	13	12	11	10	9	8	7
1981	6	4	6	4	4	2	1/31	29	28	27	26	26
1982	25	23	24	23	21	21	20	19	17	17	15	15
1983	14	13	14	13	12	11	10	8	7	6	4	4
1984	3	1	2	1	1/30	29	28	26	25	24	22	22
1985	21	19	21	20	19	18	17	16	14	14	12	12
1986	10	9	10	9	8	7	7	5	4	3	2	1/30
1987	29	28	29	28	27	26	25	24	23	22	21	20
1988	19	17	18	16	15	14	13	12	11	10	9	9
1989	7	6	7	6	5	3	3	1/31	29	29	28	28
1990	26	25	26	25	24	22	22	20	19	18	17	17
1991	15	14	15	13	13	11	11	9	8	8	6	6
1992	4	3	4	3	2	1/30	29	28	26	25	24	24
1993	24	22	24	22	21	20	19	17	16	15	14	14
1994	11	10	12	11	10	9	8	7	5	5	3	2

MOON AGE QUICK REFERENCE TABLE

SIGNIFICANT MOON AGE DAYS

YOUR OWN MOON AGE DAY

	+ Days	- Days	* Days
0	4, 6, 12, 14, 19, 21, 25, 28	9, 16, 23	0
1	5, 7, 13, 15, 20, 22, 26, 29	10, 17, 24	1
2	0, 6, 8, 14, 16, 21, 23, 27	11, 18, 25	2
3	1, 7, 9, 15, 17, 22, 24, 28	12, 19, 26	3
4	2, 8, 10, 16, 18, 23, 25, 29	13, 20, 27	4
5	0, 3, 4, 9, 11, 17, 19, 24, 26	14, 21, 28	5
6	1, 4, 5, 10, 12, 18, 20, 25, 27	15, 22, 29	6
7	2, 5, 11, 13, 19, 21, 26, 28	0, 16, 23	7
8	3, 6, 12, 14, 20, 22, 27, 29	1, 17, 24	8
9	0, 4, 7, 13, 15, 21, 23, 28	2, 18, 25	9
10	1, 5, 8, 14, 16, 22, 24, 29	3, 19, 26	10
11	0, 2, 6, 9, 15, 17, 23, 25	4, 20, 27	11
12	1, 3, 7, 10, 16, 18, 24, 26	5, 21, 28	12
13	2, 4, 8, 11, 17, 19, 25, 27	6, 22, 29	13
14	3, 5, 9, 12, 18, 20, 26, 28	0, 7, 23	14
15	4, 6, 10, 13, 19, 21, 27, 29	1, 8, 24	15
16	0, 5, 7, 11, 14, 20, 22, 28	2, 9, 25	16
17	1, 6, 8, 12, 15, 21, 23, 29	3, 10, 26	17
18	0, 2, 7, 9, 13, 16, 22, 24	4, 11, 27	18
19	1, 3, 8, 10, 14, 17, 23, 25	5, 12, 28	19
20	2,4, 9, 11, 15, 18, 24, 26	6, 13, 29	20
21	3, 5, 10, 12, 16, 19, 25, 27	0, 7, 14	21
22	4, 6, 11, 13, 17, 20, 26, 28	1, 8, 15	22
23	5, 7, 12, 14, 18, 21, 27, 29	2, 9, 16	23
24	0, 6, 8, 13, 15, 19, 22, 28	3, 10, 17	24
25	1, 7, 9, 14, 16, 20, 23, 29	4, 11, 18	25
26	0, 2, 8, 10, 15, 17, 21, 24,	5, 12, 19	26
27	1, 3, 9, 11, 16, 18, 22, 25	6, 13, 20	27
28	2, 4, 10, 12, 17, 19, 23, 26	7, 14, 21	28
29	3, 5, 11, 13, 18, 20, 24, 27	8, 15, 22	29

MOON AGE QUICK REFERENCE TABLE

The table opposite will allow you to plot the significant days on the Moon Age Day Cycle and to monitor the way they have a bearing on your own life. You will find an explanation of the Moon Age Cycles on pages 20 - 22. Once you know your own Moon Age Day, you can find it in the left-hand column of the table opposite, To the right of your Moon Age Day you will observe a series of numbers; these appear under three headings. + Days, - Days and * Days.

If you look at the Diary section of the book, immediately to the right of each day and date, the Moon Age Day number is listed. The Quick Reference Table allows you to register which Moon Age Days are significant to you. For example: if your own Moon Age Day is 5, each month you should put a + in the Diary section against Moon Age Days 0, 3, 4, 9, 11, 17, 19, 24, and 26. Jot down a - against Moon Age Days 14, 21 and 28, and a * against Moon Age Day 5. You can now follow your own personal Moon Age Cycle every day of the year.

+ Days are periods when the Moon Age Cycle is in tune with your own Moon Age Day. At this time life should be more harmonious and your emotions are likely to be running smoothly. These are good days for making decisions.

- Days find the Moon Age Cycle out of harmony with your own Moon Age Day. Avoid taking chances at these times and take life reasonably steady. Confrontation would not make sense.

* Days occur only once each Moon Age Cycle, and represent your own Moon Age Day. Such times should be excellent for taking the odd chance and for moving positively towards your objectives in life. On those rare occasions where a * day coincides with your lunar high, you would really be looking at an exceptional period and could afford to be quite bold and adventurous in your approach to life.

MOON ZODIAC SIGN TABLE 1

Month	Jan	Feb	Mar	Apr	May	Jun	Jul	Aug	Sep	Oct	Nov	Dec
1	A	D	F	J	M	O	R	U	X	a	e	i
2	A	D	G	J	M	P	R	U	X	a	e	i
3	A	D	G	J	M	P	S	V	X	a	e	m
4	A	D	G	J	M	P	S	V	Y	b	f	m
5	A	D	G	J	M	P	S	V	Y	b	f	n
6	A	D	G	J	M	P	S	V	Y	b	f	n
7	A	D	G	J	M	P	S	V	Y	b	f	n
8	A	D	G	J	M	P	S	V	Y	b	f	n
9	A	D	G	J	M	P	S	V	Y	b	f	n
10	A	E	G	J	M	P	S	V	Y	b	f	n
11	B	E	G	K	M	P	S	V	Y	b	f	n
12	B	E	H	K	N	Q	S	V	Y	b	f	n
13	B	E	H	K	N	Q	T	V	Y	b	g	n
14	B	E	H	K	N	Q	T	W	Z	d	g	n
15	B	E	H	K	N	Q	T	W	Z	d	g	n
16	B	E	H	K	N	Q	T	W	Z	d	g	n
17	B	E	H	K	N	Q	T	W	Z	d	g	n
18	B	E	H	K	N	Q	T	W	Z	d	g	n
19	B	E	H	K	N	Q	T	W	Z	d	g	n
20	B	F	H	K	N	Q	T	W	Z	d	g	n
21	C	F	H	L	N	Q	T	W	Z	d	g	n
22	C	F	I	L	O	R	T	W	Z	d	g	n
23	C	F	I	L	O	R	T	W	Z	d	i	q
24	C	F	I	L	O	R	U	X	a	e	i	q
25	C	F	I	L	O	R	U	X	a	e	i	q
26	C	F	I	L	O	R	U	X	a	e	i	q
27	C	F	I	L	O	R	U	X	a	e	i	q
28	C	F	I	L	O	R	U	X	a	e	i	q
29	C	-	I	L	O	R	U	X	a	e	i	q
30	C	-	I	L	O	R	U	X	a	e	i	q
31	D	–	I	-	O	-	U	X	-	e	-	q

Left margin label: DAY OF MONTH

LETTER

Moon Age Day	0	1	2	3	4	5	6	7	8	9	10	11	12	13
A	Ca	Aq	Aq	Aq	Pi	Pi	Ar	Ar	Ar	Ta	Ta	Ge	Ge	Ge
B	Aq	Aq	Aq	Pi	Pi	Ar	Ar	Ar	Ta	Ta	Ge	Ge	Ge	Cn
C	Aq	Aq	Pi	Pi	Ar	Ar	Ar	Ta	Ta	Ge	Ge	Ge	Cn	Cn
D	Aq	Pi	Pi	Pi	Ar	Ar	Ta	Ta	Ta	Ge	Ge	Cn	Cn	Le
E	Pi	Pi	Pi	Ar	Ar	Ta	Ta	Ta	Ge	Ge	Cn	Cn	Cn	Le
F	Pi	Pi	Ar	Ar	Ar	Ta	Ta	Ge	Ge	Cn	Cn	Cn	Le	Le
G	Pi	Ar	Ar	Ar	Ta	Ta	Ge	Ge	Ge	Cn	Cn	Le	Le	Le
H	Ar	Ar	Ar	Ta	Ta	Ge	Ge	Ge	Cn	Cn	Le	Le	Le	Vi
I	Ar	Ar	Ta	Ta	Ge	Ge	Ge	Cn	Cn	Cn	Le	Le	Vi	Vi
J	Ar	Ta	Ta	Ta	Ge	Ge	Cn	Cn	Cn	Le	Le	Vi	Vi	Vi
K	Ta	Ta	Ta	Ge	Ge	Cn	Cn	Cn	Le	Le	Vi	Vi	Vi	Li
L	Ta	Ta	Ge	Ge	Ge	Cn	Cn	Le	Le	Vi	Vi	Vi	Li	Li
M	Ta	Ge	Ge	Ge	Cn	Cn	Le	Le	Le	Vi	Vi	Li	Li	Li
N	Ge	Ge	Ge	Cn	Cn	Le	Le	Le	Vi	Vi	Li	Li	Li	Sc
O	Ge	Ge	Cn	Cn	Cn	Le	Le	Vi	Vi	Li	Li	Sc	Sc	Sc
P	Ge	Cn	Cn	Cn	Le	Le	Vi	Vi	Vi	Li	Li	Sc	Sc	Sc
Q	Cn	Cn	Cn	Le	Le	Vi	Vi	Li	Li	Sc	Sc	Sc	Sa	Sa
R	Cn	Cn	Le	Le	Le	Vi	Vi	Li	Li	Li	Sc	Sc	Sa	Sa
S	Cn	Le	Le	Le	Vi	Vi	Li	Li	Li	Sc	Sc	Sa	Sa	Sa
T	Le	Le	Le	Vi	Vi	Li	Li	Li	Sc	Sc	Sa	Sa	Sa	Ca
U	Le	Le	Vi	Vi	Li	Li	Li	Sc	Sc	Sa	Sa	Ca	Ca	Ca
V	Le	Vi	Vi	Vi	Li	Li	Sc	Sc	Sc	Sa	Sa	Ca	Ca	Ca
W	Le	Vi	Vi	Li	Li	Sc	Sc	Sa	Sa	Sa	Ca	Ca	Aq	Aq
X	Vi	Vi	Li	Li	Li	Sc	Sc	Sa	Sa	Sa	Ca	Ca	Aq	Aq
Y	Vi	Li	Li	Li	Sc	Sc	Sa	Sa	Sa	Ca	Ca	Aq	Aq	Aq
Z	Li	Li	Li	Sc	Sc	Sc	Sa	Sa	Ca	Ca	Ca	Aq	Aq	Pi
a	Li	Li	Li	Sc	Sc	Sa	Sa	Sa	Ca	Ca	Aq	Aq	Pi	Pi
b	Li	Li	Sc	Sc	Sa	Sa	Ca	Ca	Ca	Aq	Aq	Pi	Pi	Ar
d	Li	Sc	Sc	Sc	Sa	Sa	Ca	Ca	Ca	Aq	Aq	Pi	Pi	Pi
e	Sc	Sc	Sc	Sa	Sa	Ca	Ca	Aq	Aq	Aq	Pi	Pi	Ar	Ar
f	Sc	Sc	Sa	Sa	Ca	Ca	Aq	Aq	Pi	Pi	Ar	Ar	Ta	Ta
g	Sc	Sa	Sa	Ca	Ca	Aq	Aq	Pi	Pi	Pi	Ar	Ar	Ta	Ta
i	Sa	Sa	Ca	Ca	Ca	Aq	Aq	Pi	Pi	Ar	Ar	Ta	Ta	Ge
m	Sa	Sa	Ca	Ca	Aq	Aq	Aq	Pi	Pi	Ar	Ar	Ta	Ta	Ge
n	Sa	Ca	Ca	Aq	Aq	Pi	Pi	Ar	Ar	Ta	Ta	Ge	Ge	Ge
q	Ca	Ca	Aq	Aq	Pi	Pi	Ar	Ar	Ar	Ta	Ta	Ge	Ge	Ge

**Ar = Aries Ta = Taurus Ge = Gemini Cn = Cancer Le = Leo
Aq = Aquarius**

SIGN TABLE 2

14	15	16	17	18	19	20	21	22	23	24	25	26	27	28	29
Cn	Cn	Le	Le	Le	Vi	Vi	Li	Li	Li	Sc	Sc	Sa	Sa	Sa	Ca
Cn	Le	Le	Le	Vi	Vi	Li	Li	Li	Sc	Sc	Sa	Sa	Sa	Ca	Ca
Le	Le	Le	Vi	Vi	Vi	Li	Li	Sc	Sc	Sc	Sa	Sa	Ca	Ca	Ca
Le	Le	Vi	Vi	Vi	Li	Li	Sc	Sc	Sc	Sa	Sa	Ca	Ca	Aq	Aq
Le	Vi	Vi	Vi	Li	Li	Sc	Sc	Sc	Sa	Sa	Ca	Ca	Aq	Aq	Aq
Vi	Vi	Vi	Li	Li	Li	Sc	Sc	Sa	Sa	Sa	Ca	Ca	Aq	Aq	Aq
VI	Vi	Li	Li	Li	Sc	Sc	Sa	Sa	Sa	Ca	Ca	Aq	Aq	Aq	Pi
VI	Li	Li	Li	Sc	Sc	Sa	Sa	Sa	Ca	Ca	Aq	Aq	Aq	Pi	Pi
Li	Li	Li	Sc	Sc	Sc	Sa	Sa	Ca	Ca	Ca	Aq	Aq	Pi	Pi	Pi
Li	Li	Sc	Sc	Sc	Sa	Sa	Ca	Ca	Ca	Aq	Aq	Pi	Pi	Pi	Ar
Li	Sc	Sc	Sc	Sa	Sa	Ca	Ca	Ca	Aq	Aq	Pi	Pi	Pi	Ar	Ar
Li	Sc	Sc	Sa	Sa	Sa	Ca	Ca	Aq	Aq	Aq	Pi	Pi	Ar	Ar	Ar
Sc	Sc	Sa	Sa	Sa	Ca	Ca	Aq	Aq	Aq	Pi	Pi	Ar	Ar	Ar	Ta
Sc	Sa	Sa	Sa	Ca	Ca	Aq	Aq	Aq	Pi	Pi	Ar	Ar	Ar	Ta	Ta
Sa	Sa	Sa	Ca	Ca	Ca	Aq	Aq	Pi	Pi	Pi	Ar	Ar	Ta	Ta	Ta
Sa	Sa	Ca	Ca	Ca	Aq	Aq	Pi	Pi	Pi	Ar	Ar	Ta	Ta	Ta	Ge
Sa	Ca	Ca	Ca	Aq	Aq	Pi	Pi	Pi	Ar	Ar	Ta	Ta	Ta	Ge	Ge
Sa	Ca	Ca	Aq	Aq	Aq	Pi	Pi	Ar	Ar	Ar	Ta	Ta	Ge	Ge	Ge
Ca	Ca	Aq	Aq	Aq	Pi	Pi	Ar	Ar	Ar	Ta	Ta	Ge	Ge	Ge	Cn
Ca	Aq	Aq	Aq	Pi	Pi	Ar	Ar	Ar	Ta	Ta	Ge	Ge	Ge	Cn	Cn
Aq	Aq	Aq	Pi	Pi	Pi	Ar	Ar	Ta	Ta	Ta	Ge	Ge	Cn	Cn	Cn
Aq	Aq	Pi	Pi	Pi	Ar	Ar	Ta	Ta	Ta	Ge	Ge	Cn	Cn	Cn	Le
Pi	Pi	Pi	Pi	Ar	Ar	Ta	Ta	Ta	Ge	Ge	Cn	Cn	Cn	Le	Le
Pi	Pi	Pi	Ar	Ar	Ar	Ta	Ta	Ge	Ge	Ge	Cn	Cn	Le	Le	Le
Pi	Pi	Ar	Ar	Ar	Ta	Ta	Ge	Ge	Ge	Cn	Cn	Le	Le	Le	Vi
Pi	Pi	Ar	Ar	Ar	Ta	Ta	Ge	Ge	Ge	Cn	Cn	Le	Le	Le	Vi
Ar	Ar	Ar	Ar	Ta	Ta	Ge	Ge	Ge	Cn	Cn	Cn	Le	Le	Vi	Vi
Ar	Ar	Ar	Ta	Ta	Ta	Ge	Ge	Cn	Cn	Cn	Le	Le	Vi	Vi	Vi
Ar	Ar	Ta	Ta	Ge	Ge	Ge	Cn	Cn	Cn	Le	Le	Vi	Vi	Vi	Li
Ta	Ta	Ta	Ge	Ge	Ge	Cn	Cn	Cn	Le	Le	Le	Vi	Vi	Li	Li
Ge	Ta	Ge	Ge	Ge	Cn	Cn	Cn	Le	Le	Le	Vi	Vi	Li	Li	Li
Ge	Ta	Ge	Ge	Cn	Cn	Cn	Le	Le	Le	Vi	Vi	Li	Li	Li	Sc
Ge	Ge	Ge	Cn	Cn	Cn	Le	Le	Vi	Vi	Vi	Li	Li	Sc	Sc	Sc
Ge	Ge	Cn	Cn	Cn	Le	Le	Le	Vi	Vi	Vi	Li	Li	Sc	Sc	Sa
Cn	Ge	Cn	Cn	Le	Le	Le	Vi	Vi	Vi	Li	Li	Sc	Sc	Sc	Sa
Cn	Cn	Cn	Le	Le	Le	Vi	Vi	Li	Li	Li	Sc	Sc	Sa	Sa	Sa

Vi = Virgo Li = Libra Sc = Scorpio Sa = Sagittarius Ca = Capricorn Pi = Pisces

MOON SIGNS

MOON IN ARIES

You have a strong imagination and a desire to do things in your own way. Showing no lack of courage you can forge your own path through life with great determination.

Originality is one of your most important attributes, you are seldom stuck for an idea though your mind is very changeable and more attention might be given over to one job at once. Few have the ability to order you around and you can be quite quick tempered. A calm and relaxed attitude is difficult for you to adopt but because you put tremendous pressure on your nervous system it is vitally important for you to forget about the cut and thrust of life from time to time. It would be fair to say that you rarely get the rest that you both need and deserve and becaue of this there is a chance that your health could break down from time to time.

Emotionally speaking you can be a bit of a mess if you don't talk to the folks that you are closest to and work out how you really feel about things. Once you discover that there are people willing to help you there is suddenly less necessity for trying to tackle everything yourself.

MOON IN TAURUS

The Moon in Taurus at the time you were born gives you a courteous and friendly manner that is likely to assure you of many friends.

The good things in life mean a great deal to you for Taurus is an Earth sign and delights in experiences that please the senses. This probably makes you a lover of good food and drink and might also mean that you have to spend time on the bathroom scales balancing the delight of a healthy appetite with that of looking good which is equally important to you.

Emotionally you are fairly stable and once you have opted for a set of standards you are inclined to stick to them because Taurus is a Fixed sign and doesn't respond particularly well to change. Intuition also plays an important part in your life.

MOON IN GEMINI

The Moon in the sign of Gemini gives a warm-hearted character, full of sympathy and usually ready to help those in difficulty. In some matters you are very reserved, whilst at other
times you are articulate and chatty: this is part of the paradox
of Gemini which always brings duplicity to the nature. The
knowledge you possess of local and national affairs is very
good, this strengthens and enlivens your intellect making you
good company and endowing you with many friends. Most of
the people with whom you mix have a high opinion of you and
will stand ready to leap to your defence, not that this is
generally necessary for although you are not martial by nature,
you are more than capable of defending yourself verbally.

Travel plays an important part in your life and the naturally inquisitive quality of your mind allows you to benefit greatly
from changes in scenery. The more you mix with people from
different cultures and backgrounds the greater your interest in
life becomes and intellectual stimulus is the meat and drink of
the Gemini individual.

You can gain through reading and writing as well as the cul-
tivation of artistic pursuits but you do need plenty of rest in
order to avoid fatigue.

MOON IN CANCER

Moon in Cancer at the time of birth is a most fortunate position
since the sign of Cancer is the Moon's natural home. This
means that the qualities of compassion and understanding
given by the Moon are especially enhanced in your nature and
you cope quite well with emotional pressures that would bother
others. You are friendly and sociably inclined. Domestic tasks
don't really bother you and your greatest love is likely to be for
home and family. Your surroundings are particularly important and you hate squalor and filth.

Your basic character, although at times changeable like the
Moon itself, depends upon symmetry. Little wonder then that
you are almost certain to have a love of music and poetry. Not
surprising either that you do all within your power to make
your surroundings comfortable and harmonious, not only for
yourself, but on behalf of the folk who mean so much to you.

MOON IN LEO

You are especially ambitious and self-confident. The best qualities of both the Moon and the Sign of Leo come together here to ensure that you are warm-hearted and fair, characteristics that are almost certain to show through no matter what other planetary positions your chart contains.

You certainly don't lack the ability to organise, either yourself or those around you, and you invariably rise to a position of responsibility no matter what you decide to do with your life. Perhaps it is just as well because you don't enjoy being an'also ran' and would much rather be an important part of a small organisation than a menial in a larger one.

In love you are likely to be lucky and happy provided that youput in that extra bit of effort and you can be relied upon to build comfortable home surroundings for yourself and also those for whom you feel a particular responsibility. It is likely that you will have a love of pleasure and sport and perhaps a fondness for music and literature. Life brings you many rewards, though most of them are as a direct result of the effort that you are able to put in on your own behalf. All the same you are inclined to be more lucky than average and will usually make the best of any given circumstance.

MOON IN VIRGO

This position of the Moon endows you with good mental abilities and a keen receptive memory. By nature you are probably quite reserved, nevertheless you have many friends, especially of the opposite sex, and you gain a great deal as a result of these associations. Marital relationships need to be discussed carefully and kept as harmonious as possible because personal attachments can be something of a problem to you if sufficient attention is not given to the way you handle them.

You are not ostentatious or pretentious, two characteristics that are sure to improve your popularity. Talented and persevering you possess artistic qualities and are a good homemaker. Earning your honours through genuine merit you can work long and hard towards your objectives but probably show very little pride in your genuine achievements. Many short journeys will be undertaken in your life.

MOON IN LIBRA

With the Moon in Libra you have a popular nature and don't find it particularly difficult to make friends. Most folk like you, probably more than you think, and all get-together's would be more fun with you present. Libra, for all its good points, is not the most stable of astrological signs and as a result your emotions can prove to be a little unstable too. Although the Moon in Libra is generally said to be good for love and marriage, the position of the Sun, and also the Rising Sign, in your own birth chart will have a greater than usual bearing on your emotional and loving qualities.

You cannot live your life in isolation and must rely on other people, who are likely to play an important part in your decision making. Cooperation is crucial for you because Libra represents the 'balance' of life that can only be achieved through harmonious relationships. An offshoot of this fact is that you do not enjoy being disliked and, like all Librans are friendly to practically everybody.

Conformity is not always easy for you, because Libra is an Air sign and likes to go its own way.

MOON IN SCORPIO

Some people might call you a little pushy, in fact all you really want to do is live your life to the full, and to protect yourself and your family from the pressures of life that you recognise all too readily. You should avoid giving the impression of being sarcastic or too impulsive, at the same time using your energies wisely and in a constructive manner.

Nobody could doubt your courage which is great, and you invariably achieve what you set out to do, by force of personality as well as by the effort that you are able to put in. You are fond of mystery and are probably quite perceptive as to the outcome of situations and events.

Problems can arise in your relationships with members of the opposite sex, so before you commit yourself emotionally it is very important to examine your motives carefully and ensure that the little demon, jealousy, always a problem with Scorpio positions, does not cloud your judgement in love matches. You need to travel and can make gains as a result.

MOON IN SAGITTARIUS

The Moon is Sagittarius helps to make you a generous individual with humanitarian qualities and a kind heart. Restlessness may be an endemic part of your character for your mind is seldom still. Perhaps because of this you have an overwhelming need for change that could lead you to several major moves during your adult life. You are probably a reasonably sporting sort of person and not afraid to stand your ground on the occasions when you know that you are correct in your judgement. What you have to say goes right to the heart of the matter and your intuition is very good.

At work you are quick and efficient in whatever you choose to do, and because you are versatile you make an ideal employee. Ideally you need work that is intellectually demanding because you are no drudge and would not enjoy tedious routines. In relationships you anger quickly if faced with stupidity or deception, though you are just as quick to forgive and forget. Emotionally there are times when you allow your heart to rule your head.

MOON IN CAPRICORN

Born with the Moon in Capricorn, you are popular and may come into the public eye in one way or another. Your administrative ability is good and you are a capable worker. The watery Moon is not entirely at home in the Earth sign of Capricorn and as a result difficulties can be experienced, especially in the early years of life. Some initial lack of creative ability and indecision has to be overcome before the true qualities of patience and perseverance inherent in Capricorn can show through.

If caution is exercised in financial affairs you can accumulate wealth with the passing of time but you will always have to be careful about forming any partnerships because you are open to deception more than most. Under such circumstances you would be well-advised to gain professional advice before committing yourself. Many people with the Moon in Capricorn take a healthy interest in social or welfare work. The organisational skills that you have, together with a genuine sympathy for others, means that you are suited to this kind of career.

MOON IN AQUARIUS

With the Moon in Aquarius you are an active and agreeable person with a friendly easy going sort of nature. Being sympathetic to the needs of other people you flourish best in an easy going atmosphere. You are broad-minded, just, and open to suggestion, though as with all faces of Aquarius the Moon here brings an unconventional quality that not everyone would find easy to understand.

You have a liking for anything strange and curious as well a fascination for old articles and places. Journeys to such locations would suit you doubly because you love to travel and can gain a great deal from the trips that you make. Political, scientific and educational work might all be of interest to you and you would gain from a career in some new and exciting branch of science or technology.

Money-wise, you make gains through innovation as much as by concentration and it isn't unusual to find lunar Aquarians tackling more than one job at the same time. In love you are honest and kind.

MOON IN PISCES

This position assures you of a kind sympathetic nature, somewhat retiring at times but always taking account of others and doing your best to help them. As with all planets in Pisces there is bound to be some misfortune on the way through life. In particular relationships of a personal nature can be problematic and often through no real fault of your own. Inevitably though suffering brings a better understanding, both of yourself and of the world around you. With a fondness for travel you appreciate beauty and harmony wherever you encounter them and hate disorder and strife.

You are probably very fond of literature and could make a good writer or speaker yourself. The imagination that you possess can be readily translated into creativity and you might come across as an incurable romantic. Being naturally receptive your intuition is strong, in many cases verging on a mediumistic quality that sets you apart from the world. You might not be rich in hard cash terms and yet the gifts that you possess and display, when used properly, are worth more than gold.

THE ASTRAL DIARY

How the diagrams work

Through the *picture diagrams* in the Astral Diary I want to help you to plot your year. With them you can see where the positive and negative aspects will be found each month. To make the most of them all you have to do is remember where and when!

Let me show you how they work . . .

THE MONTH AT A GLANCE

Just as there are twelve separate Zodiac Signs, so Astrologers believe that each sign has twelve separate aspects to life. Each of the twelve segments relates to a different personal aspect. I number and list them all every month as a key so that their meanings are always clear.

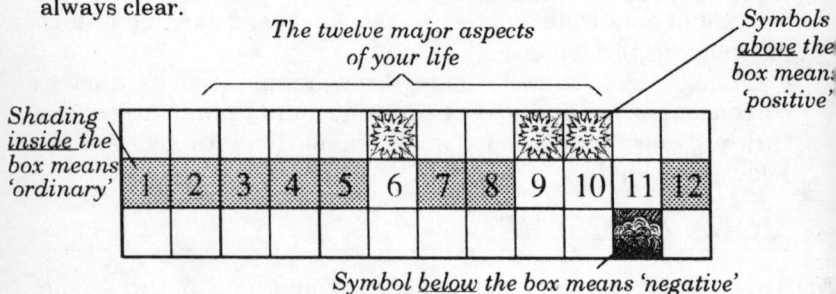

*The twelve major aspects
of your life*

*Symbols
above the
box means
'positive'*

*Shading
inside the
box means
'ordinary'*

| 1 | 2 | 3 | 4 | 5 | 6 | 7 | 8 | 9 | 10 | 11 | 12 |

Symbol below the box means 'negative'

I have designed this chart to show you how and when these twelve different aspects are being influenced throughout the year. When the number rests comfortably in its shaded box, nothing out of the ordinary is to be expected. However, when a box turns white, then you should expect influences to become active in this area of your life. Where the influence is positive I have raised a smiling sun above its number. Where it is a negative, I hang a little rain cloud beneath it.

YOUR ENERGY RHYTHM CHART

On the opposite page is a picture diagram in which I am linking your zodiac group to the rhythm of the moon. In doing this I have calculated when you will be gaining strength from its influence and equally when you may be weakened by it.

If you think of yourself as being like the tides of the ocean then you may understand how your own energies must rise and fall too. And if you understand how it works and when it is working, then you can better organise your activities to achieve more and get things done more easily.

YOUR ENERGY-RHYTHM CHART

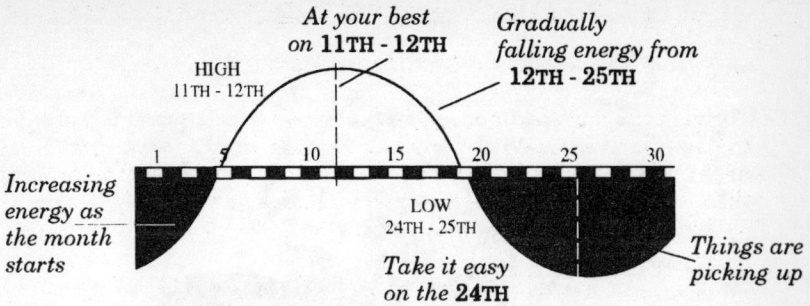

At your best on 11TH - 12TH

Gradually falling energy from 12TH - 25TH

HIGH
11TH - 12TH

Increasing energy as the month starts

1   5   10   15   20   25   30

LOW
24TH - 25TH

Take it easy on the 24TH

Things are picking up

MOVING PICTURE SCREEN
Measured every week
LOVE, LUCK, MONEY & VITALITY

I hope that the diagram below offers more than a little fun. It is very easy to use. The bars move across the scale to give you some idea of the strength of opportunities open to you in each of the four areas. If LOVE stands at plus 4, then get out and put yourself about, because in terms of romance, things should be going your way. When the bar moves backwards then the opportunities are weakening and when it enters the negative scale, then romance should not be at the top of your list.

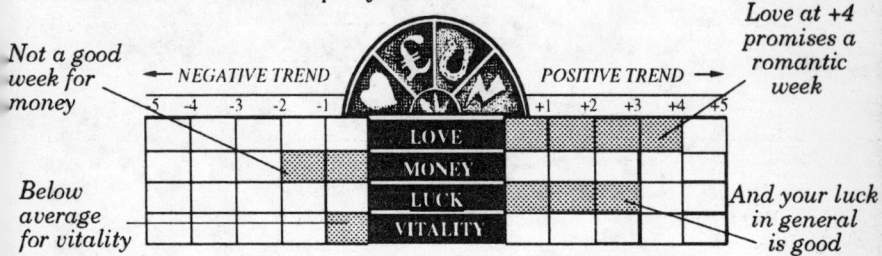

Love at +4 promises a romantic week

Not a good week for money

← *NEGATIVE TREND*   *POSITIVE TREND* →

-5 -4 -3 -2 -1   +1 +2 +3 +4 +5

LOVE
MONEY
LUCK
VITALITY

Below average for vitality

And your luck in general is good

And Finally:

am ....

pm ....

The two lines that are left blank in each daily entry of the Astral Diary are for your own personal use. You may find them ideal for keeping a check on birthdays or appointments, though it could be an idea to make notes from the astrological trends and diagrams a few weeks in advance. Some of the lines carry a key, as above. These days are important because they indicate the working of 'astrological cycles' in your life. The 'key' readings show how best you can act, react or simply work within them for greater success.

1993

YOUR MONTH AT A GLANCE

The twelve numbered boxes represent the important areas in your life.
The key to the numbers you will find beneath the panel. A Sun above
the number indicates that opportunities are around. A Cloud below
the number, that you should be a bit defensive. Nothing above or
below and life will be pretty ordinary.

1	2	3	4	5	6	7	8	9	10	11	12

KEY

1 Strength of Personality	7 One to One Relationships
2 Personal Finance	8 Questioning, Thinking & Deciding
3 Useful Information Gathering	9 External Influences / Education
4 Domestic Affairs	10 Career Aspirations
5 Pleasure & Romance	11 Teamwork Activities
6 Effective Work & Health	12 Unconscious Impulses

OCTOBER HIGHS AND LOWS

Here, I show how the rhythm of the Moon will affect you this month.
Like the tide, your energies and abilities will rise and fall with its pattern. When it is above the date line, go-for-it. When it is below the
line you should be resting.

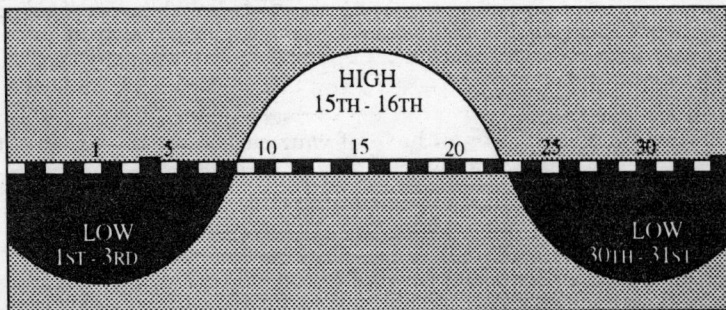

HIGH
15TH - 16TH

1   5   10   15   20   25   30

LOW
1ST - 3RD

LOW
30TH - 31ST

4 MONDAY
Moon Age Day 18 • Moon Sign Taurus

am ....

pm ....

Expect to be very busy today. Emotional issues are more or less certain to surface at some stage throughout the day, though they should have only a limited part to play in your thinking. Be prepared to take some decisive action, even if it means letting certain people down.

5 TUESDAY
Moon Age Day 19 • Moon Sign Taurus

am ....

pm ....

News received today could clear up some complicated situations that have been holding you back, particularly regarding your finances. There is a slight emphasis on your own sense of security at the present time, so you will be anxious to look out the support of friends.

6 WEDNESDAY
Moon Age Day 20 • Moon Sign Gemini

am ....

pm ....

Changes in routines can do much to lift your spirits today. Variety is what you really need and you could even be discussing the possibility of a journey that you have been looking forward to. Friends are full of interesting news, which in itself is enough to make you feel good.

7 THURSDAY
Moon Age Day 21 • Moon Sign Gemini

am ....

pm ....

Examine the view that you have of your career prospects, and if necessary be prepared to make changes. Things generally are unlikely to remain exactly the same as they have been in the past and for now you should relish the potential for some exciting alternatives, socially and practically.

8 FRIDAY

Moon Age Day 22 • Moon Sign Cancer

am ....

pm ....

You have a great appetite for change and diversity. Life is on the move and you are only too anxious to make the most of all opportunities as they occur. Luxuries are important and it is likely that you will be able to find the time to cosset yourself a little. Confidence begins to grow.

9 SATURDAY

Moon Age Day 23 • Moon Sign Cancer

am ....

pm ....

Details are easy to overlook in connection with personal matters of any sort, all the more reason to watch carefully and not to allow a busy schedule to prevent you from keeping one eye on your love life. This is not a good period for being too hasty though, or for forcing issues of any sort.

10 SUNDAY

Moon Age Day 24 • Moon Sign Leo

am ....

pm ....

Trends are slightly less favourable today and you may have to allow other people to get their own way more than you really think is good for either them or you. News that comes in the form of gossip is likely to be a little unreliable, so take it with a pinch of salt.

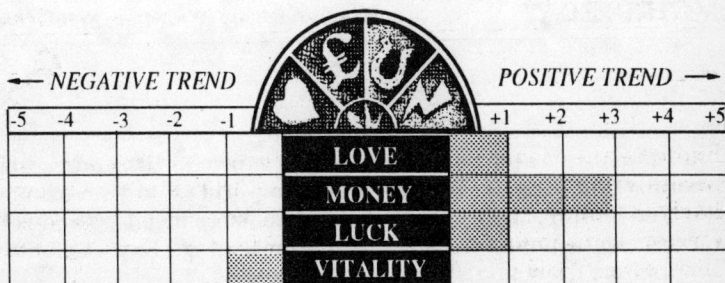

← *NEGATIVE TREND*   *POSITIVE TREND* →

-5	-4	-3	-2	-1		+1	+2	+3	+4	+5
					LOVE					
					MONEY					
					LUCK					
					VITALITY					

11 MONDAY

Moon Age Day 25 • Moon Sign Leo

am ....

pm ....

A socially prominent day, and one that should find you actively pushing your own interests to the top of other people's agendas. New contacts are a possibility at the present time, though any minor setbacks could be as a result of slightly depleted financial reserves, so spend wisely.

12 TUESDAY

Moon Age Day 26 • Moon Sign Leo

am ....

pm ....

You recognise the need for a long, hard look at life. Unsatisfactory elements need careful consideration and possibly some discussion with your nearest and dearest. Once you have made up your mind, start putting changes into action as quickly as you can. New incentives are quite vital.

13 WEDNESDAY

Moon Age Day 27 • Moon Sign Virgo

am ....

pm ....

Long-term indications, especially those of a financial nature, should be looking especially good at present. It is important to maintain a positive and optimistic attitude now, and not to allow the less than positive opinions and attitudes of those close to you to get in the way.

14 THURSDAY

Moon Age Day 28 • Moon Sign Virgo

am ....

pm ....

The lunar high approaches, and does much to lift your spirits generally, allowing you to respond to the world at large much more as a true Libran should. Life begins to feel more inspiring and petty worries can be put to one side for the time being. Expect plenty of favours from friends.

15 FRIDAY
Moon Age Day 0 • Moon Sign Libra

am ....

pm ....

Generosity is your middle name at present and it is to be hoped that you do not act so unselfishly that you forget about your own interests completely on the way. In terms of leisure time, other people appear to be determined to put you in the spotlight, which should not worry you at all.

16 SATURDAY
Moon Age Day 1 • Moon Sign Libra

am ....

pm ....

Venus enters your own sign of Libra now, always a fortunate situation since it is also your personal ruling planet. This should open up the most positive part of the month as far as your love life is concerned, bringing new opportunities for the single and contentment for the settled Libran. Effort is still required however.

17 SUNDAY
Moon Age Day 2 • Moon Sign Scorpio

am ....

pm ....

Other people are likely to be singing your praises at present, and there would be no harm at all in benefiting from the popularity that you enjoy now. In most respects, immediate action is the best response, though you should ensure that friends and relatives alike understand your intentions.

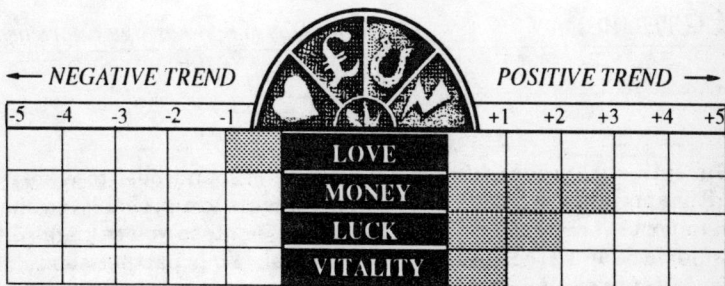

← NEGATIVE TREND						POSITIVE TREND →				
-5	-4	-3	-2	-1		+1	+2	+3	+4	+5
					LOVE					
					MONEY					
					LUCK					
					VITALITY					

18 MONDAY
Moon Age Day 3 • Moon Sign Scorpio

am ....

pm ....

Use today to discuss all important issues, and to get the permission of superiors to take the sort of action that you know would be providential. Some luck can come in an association with travel, either in reality, or even relating to journeys that are no further on than the planning stage.

19 TUESDAY
Moon Age Day 4 • Moon Sign Sagittarius

am ....

pm ....

Your practical outlook is now fairly positive and you are certainly in the right frame of mind to be attracting money to yourself. As always, you are generally willing to share any honours that are in the offing, though you could also feel that your own successes are not being recognised enough.

20 WEDNESDAY
Moon Age Day 5 • Moon Sign Sagittarius

am ....

pm ....

Now you are looking for a feeling of domestic harmony and the sort of togetherness that you relish in personal relationships. You do have a tendency to become complacent about professional issues, but must do your best not to let things slide. New contacts can bring some important news.

21 THURSDAY
Moon Age Day 6 • Moon Sign Capricorn

am ....

pm ....

Domestic disagreements are inclined to respond best to a softly-softly approach on your part. Disagreements are probably not half as important as they appear to be at first sight, so you can afford to stand back and at least try to be impartial. Your partner should be very attentive at present.

22 FRIDAY

Moon Age Day 7 • Moon Sign Capricorn

am ....

pm ....

There could be cause for some celebrations now. For most Librans, romance is an important part of the scenario right now, as loving Venus begins to exert here full force in your own Sun sign. Social issues are apt to seem more important than some of the pressing practical aspects of your life.

23 SATURDAY

Moon Age Day 8 • Moon Sign Aquarius

am ....

pm ....

The Sun now enters your solar second house, which is likely to bring something of a boost in financial terms over the next month or so. Your attitudes to spending are now more liberated in some ways and you should not allow yourself to be thwarted by the opinions of less positive people.

24 SUNDAY

Moon Age Day 9 • Moon Sign Aquarius

am ....

pm ....

Home life is now a hive of activity. This would be the best time of all for thinking about alterations of any sort, or for getting things organised so that you can face the coming winter in the most comfortable way possible. Discussions with family members can prove to be very useful.

← NEGATIVE TREND　　　　　　　*POSITIVE TREND →*

-5	-4	-3	-2	-1		+1	+2	+3	+4	+5
					LOVE					
					MONEY					
					LUCK					
					VITALITY					

25 MONDAY
Moon Age Day 10 • Moon Sign Pisces

am ....

pm ....

There should be little in the way of pressure for you at the moment, though it is possible that you will be having some fairly serious discussions relating to your personal and romantic life. It really is worth talking things over at length today, not to mention being willing to listen.

26 TUESDAY
Moon Age Day 11 • Moon Sign Pisces

am ....

pm ....

Assistance now comes from some fairly unexpected quarters. You are feeling fairly vigorous now and well able to cope with the sort of pressures that may have been inclined to get you down in the fairly recent past. In a social sense, don't be surprised if you are pushed to the forefront.

27 WEDNESDAY
Moon Age Day 12 • Moon Sign Pisces

am ....

pm ....

You may need to admit your responsibility for a mistake or two recently, most likely born out of impetuosity on your part. It is unlikely that any real damage has been done however and you can soon put matters right by relying on the help and advice of a professional, or even a knowledgeable friend.

28 THURSDAY
Moon Age Day 13 • Moon Sign Aries

am ....

pm ....

Now you have to contend with the slightly negative qualities of the lunar low. Your physical vitality could take a slight nose-dive, all the more reason to concentrate on matters cerebral for the moment. Even in the brain department, it's a case of planning but not of implementing just yet.

29 FRIDAY

Moon Age Day 14 • Moon Sign Aries

am ....

pm ....

There are signs about that are saying you should be prepared to take life rather steadily now, even though in some ways that is the last thing you want to do. Major decisions will still have to wait for a while, even though in a more social sense it appears that things are happening.

30 SATURDAY

Moon Age Day 15 • Moon Sign Taurus

am ....

pm ....

Slight financial hold-ups need not prevent the general forward movement that you are able to enjoy at present. There are significant rewards about at present, just as long as you are willing to take the odd chance. Less adventurous Librans will want to wait for a day or two.

31 SUNDAY

Moon Age Day 16 • Moon Sign Taurus

am ....

pm ....

Although you could now be inclined to take a rather trivial approach to what could be fairly important emotional matters, be prepared to hear the truth as it is seen by others. Taking people or situations for granted is not to be recommended at present. Financial news could cheer you up later.

← *NEGATIVE TREND*   *POSITIVE TREND* →

-5	-4	-3	-2	-1		+1	+2	+3	+4	+5
					LOVE					
					MONEY					
					LUCK					
					VITALITY					

1993

YOUR MONTH AT A GLANCE

The twelve numbered boxes represent the important areas in your life. The key to the numbers you will find beneath the panel. A Sun above the number indicates that opportunities are around. A Cloud below the number, that you should be a bit defensive. Nothing above or below and life will be pretty ordinary.

☼							☼				☼
1	2	3	4	5	6	7	8	9	10	11	12

KEY

1 Strength of Personality
2 Personal Finance
3 Useful Information Gathering
4 Domestic Affairs
5 Pleasure & Romance
6 Effective Work & Health

7 One to One Relationships
8 Questioning, Thinking & Deciding
9 External Influences / Education
10 Career Aspirations
11 Teamwork Activities
12 Unconscious Impulses

NOVEMBER HIGHS AND LOWS

Here, I show how the rhythm of the Moon will affect you this month. Like the tide, your energies and abilities will rise and fall with its pattern. When it is above the date line, go-for-it. When it is below the line you should be resting.

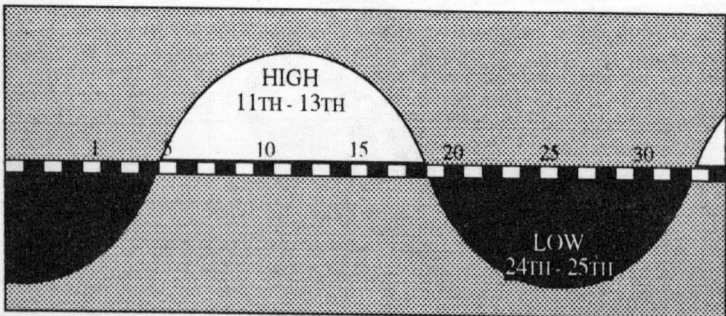

HIGH
11TH - 13TH

LOW
24TH - 25TH

1 MONDAY
Moon Age Day 17 • Moon Sign Taurus

am ....

pm ....

There could be a few issues about at present that you find to be quite dissatisfying. Perhaps you need to be reminded that things are a good deal better than you imagine. Take some timely advice over domestic issues of one sort or another and don't be put off by temporary problems.

2 TUESDAY
Moon Age Day 18 • Moon Sign Gemini

am ....

pm ....

There are revisions and changes to be considered, particularly where travel issues are concerned. Life should be fairly pleasurable all the same, with advantages coming from a host of different directions. Friends have opinions that could seem distinctly odd, though you should wait and see.

3 WEDNESDAY
Moon Age Day 19 • Moon Sign Gemini

am ....

pm ....

With Venus now very comfortable in its own rulership of Libra, you should be experiencing a significantly positive quality to all aspects of love and romance. Your nature is attractive to outsiders and also to people you know very well. The only real danger might be in allowing good times to get in the way of practicalities.

4 THURSDAY
Moon Age Day 20 • Moon Sign Cancer

am ....

pm ....

All professional issues in your life should now show indications of positive times ahead. Information received is apt to lead to lucky breaks of one sort or another. Most important of all is the level of understanding that can now exist, even with people who have not been important before.

5 FRIDAY
Moon Age Day 21 • Moon Sign Cancer

am ....

pm ....

There is much give and take around, and possibly a high degree of compromise. Benefits at work come as a result of significantly better understanding, both on your part and with regard to people in your immediate vicinity. Instructions are clear and concise, and opportunities abound.

6 SATURDAY
Moon Age Day 22 • Moon Sign Cancer

am ....

pm ....

The favours you may be expecting from friends should be forthcoming today, even if they do not actually turn out as you may have expected. There is likely to be a great deal of fun and a spirit of friendship that can lift the weekend into a different dimension. Don't look too deeply into situations.

7 SUNDAY
Moon Age Day 23 • Moon Sign Leo

am ....

pm ....

Things may go a little haywire today, with some possible rebuffs from friends and acquaintances. Sometimes there is no accounting for the way that people behave and unless you know for certain that you have done something to upset them, it might be best to simply wait and see what happens later in the day.

← *NEGATIVE TREND*　　　　　　　*POSITIVE TREND* →

-5	-4	-3	-2	-1			+1	+2	+3	+4	+5
					LOVE						
					MONEY						
					LUCK						
					VITALITY						

8 MONDAY
Moon Age Day 24 • Moon Sign Leo

am ....

pm ....

Finances look stronger for a while now, which could lead to a spending spree that might be ill-advised. You would be better off piling up your cash for the next few days and observing the way that situations are going. That way you could end up getting much more for your money in the long-run.

9 TUESDAY
Moon Age Day 25 • Moon Sign Virgo

am ....

pm ....

Venus now enters your solar second house, and some of the emphasis begins to shift in the direction of luxuries that you are looking for in your life. Your eye is now also easily transfixed by what you consider to be beautiful, and since others respect your judgements in such matters, you can make your opinions count.

10 WEDNESDAY
Moon Age Day 26 • Moon Sign Virgo

am ....

pm ....

There are important indications on the financial front, though as so many of them are fairly subtle in character it would be an idea to keep your eyes open. Very little of life is obvious at the moment and it is a good thing that you are the sort of person who can easily monitor the undertones.

11 THURSDAY
Moon Age Day 27 • Moon Sign Libra

am ....

pm ....

The Moon returns to your own sign of Libra, bringing a very cheerful frame of mind. Be careful that you are not so keen on results that you begin to force issues that would be better left to sort themselves out. Despite the positive trends, this would not be an ideal time to interfere.

12 FRIDAY

Moon Age Day 28 • Moon Sign Libra

am ....

pm ....

Attention can now be paid to furthering your ambitions, since all that you need to start life rolling along in your direction is with and around you. In professional matters you can really begin to shine, though personal relationships need more thinking about and greater subtlety in your handling of them.

13 SATURDAY

Moon Age Day 0 • Moon Sign Scorpio

am ....

pm ....

A more assertive approach now becomes possible as Mars enters your solar third house. It is likely that you become very outspoken regarding issues that have been close to your heart for some time. Don't allow this trend to go too far, or you could end up alienating people who are very useful.

14 SUNDAY

Moon Age Day 1 • Moon Sign Scorpio

am ....

pm ....

Try to avoid becoming worrisome about issues that you can neither control nor alter. Life should be looking after you fairly well at present, though you do show a tendency to be anxious about incidents that probably have little validity where the broader issues of your life are concerned.

← *NEGATIVE TREND*   *POSITIVE TREND* →

-5	-4	-3	-2	-1			+1	+2	+3	+4	+5
					LOVE						
					MONEY						
					LUCK						
					VITALITY						

15 MONDAY   *Moon Age Day 2 • Moon Sign Sagittarius*

am ....

pm ....

For once you are very reluctant to compromise, a situation that you don't really know how to deal with since it shows itself so rarely in your life. You certainly need to think carefully before you speak, because without your usual compromise, you are naked to the responses of less than kind individuals.

16 TUESDAY   *Moon Age Day 3 • Moon Sign Sagittarius*

am ....

pm ....

A slightly hectic phase now commences, especially with regard to developments in your work life. All the same, you should do your best to take fences one at a time since there are no prizes for rushing at present. Romantic potential is more encouraging now than it may have been for some time.

17 WEDNESDAY   *Moon Age Day 4 • Moon Sign Capricorn*

am ....

pm ....

This would be a favourable interlude to resolve financial problems of one sort or another. You also might think about reviewing some of your own personal plans, one or two of which may not be yielding the fruit that you had hoped. However, once you sort out your priorities, everything will be back on line.

18 THURSDAY   *Moon Age Day 5 • Moon Sign Capricorn*

am ....

pm ....

Domestic issues are now in the spotlight, and it is possible that you will choose the present time for family discussions that can allow you to monitor the way that your nearest and dearest are really feeling about life. There are critics about, though much of what they are saying is nonsensical.

19 FRIDAY
Moon Age Day 6 • Moon Sign Aquarius

am ....

pm ....

Minor disagreements about money should not be allowed to alter your own way of dealing with situations, even though it is vital to allow others to have their say. Small irritations are almost certain at present, but are only as restricting as you allow them to be, dependent on your state of mind.

20 SATURDAY
Moon Age Day 7 • Moon Sign Aquarius

am ....

pm ....

At last some of your more favoured pet projects are beginning to bear fruit, after a week that may not have appeared to be especially dynamic. Saturday should give you the opportunity to get other people involved in your own schemes socially, though romantic proposals may take a back seat.

21 SUNDAY
Moon Age Day 8 • Moon Sign Aquarius

am ....

pm ....

Although present trends favour a general lifting of pressure, and especially so where financial matters are concerned, even the fact that this is Sunday could hold you up in a number of ways. All the more reason to settle back and accept the rest and relaxation that you probably need so badly.

<— NEGATIVE TREND   POSITIVE TREND —>

	-5	-4	-3	-2	-1		+1	+2	+3	+4	+5
LOVE				▒	▒						
MONEY							▒				
LUCK							▒	▒			
VITALITY							▒				

22 MONDAY
Moon Age Day 9 • Moon Sign Pisces

am ....

pm ....

The Sun now enters your solar third house, and you begin to become more socially prominent, persuasive and influential. Positive ideas begin to find a better means of expression generally and results are the conclusion. It is still vital that you resist any tendency to rush things for the time being.

23 TUESDAY
Moon Age Day 10 • Moon Sign Pisces

am ....

pm ....

You can find satisfaction galore at work, simply as a result of a job well done. Loved ones can be very helpful once the workaday routines have been taken care of and there are a number of ways to begin feeling that life is on course more than you may have consciously felt recently.

24 WEDNESDAY
Moon Age Day 11 • Moon Sign Aries

am ....

pm ....

Be prepared for the temporary set-backs brought about by the presence of the lunar low in your general routines. You could be feeling rather let down in a financial sense, though it has to be said that you are probably looking at things in a rather negative way and will not be helping yourself.

25 THURSDAY
Moon Age Day 12 • Moon Sign Aries

am ....

pm ....

This is a good stage to be planning, but it may not be the most propitious phase for actually putting your plans into action. Expect a low-key sort of day, though one that offers plenty of time to mull things over, particularly in a personal sense. This is fine, but don't dwell on problems.

26 FRIDAY
Moon Age Day 13 • Moon Sign Aries

am ....

pm ....

It is rare for a Libran to be accused of being too practical in their approach to life, though though this could easily be the case at present. Meanwhile, opinions amongst your circle of friends are inclined to differ markedly, possibly leaving you in the position of deciding between them for a few days.

27 SATURDAY
Moon Age Day 14 • Moon Sign Taurus

am ....

pm ....

Look out for some drama in your romantic life and deal with the situation quickly and decisively. You are not likely to be taking outsiders into your confidence very much at the moment and even friends could find you to be more aloof than usual. Take the opportunity to embrace new starts.

28 SUNDAY
Moon Age Day 15 • Moon Sign Taurus

am ....

pm ....

Where money is owed to you take the opportunity offered by today to call it in. There is no reason why your own life should be held back simply because others are not getting their own financial act together. Leisure pursuits could be something of a disappointment unless you put in real effort.

← *NEGATIVE TREND*   *POSITIVE TREND* →

-5	-4	-3	-2	-1		+1	+2	+3	+4	+5
					LOVE					
					MONEY					
					LUCK					
					VITALITY					

29 MONDAY

Moon Age Day 16 • Moon Sign Gemini

am ....

pm ....

Take the initiative with people in authority and don't allow your plans to be held back on those occasions when it is possible to take the lead. A resolution to financial pressures would probably be more than welcome and appears to be possible, in part at least, quite soon.

30 TUESDAY

Moon Age Day 17 • Moon Sign Gemini

am ....

pm ....

As the month draws to a close the more restless side of your nature begins to show itself to the world at large. You are certainly ready for something new, and for a dose of excitement that only you can find for yourself. In conversation, serious topics tend to predominate.

1 WEDNESDAY

Moon Age Day 18 • Moon Sign Gemini

am ....

pm ....

There is little doubt that you are out to impress others as much as you can right now, but don't take any aspect of your own nature for granted either. Career matters should be looking fairly promising, whilst your domestic arrangements can be a source of genuine joy at present.

2 THURSDAY

Moon Age Day 19 • Moon Sign Cancer

am ....

pm ....

With Mars now settled in your solar third house of communication, you are certainly on the ball when it comes to a discussion of any sort. That usually affable nature is now inclined to be much more assertive, though you also show an increase in curiosity and the desire to learn. All good incentives for a fuller life.

3 FRIDAY
Moon Age Day 20 • Moon Sign Cancer

am ....

pm ....

Now Venus, your ruling planet, enters the third house, indicating that journeys of almost any sort can be of special interest. Others will find you great fun to be with at this time and everyday life should be running fairly smoothly. The days ahead offer a great degree of self-choice and good general incentives.

4 SATURDAY
Moon Age Day 21 • Moon Sign Leo

am ....

pm ....

You could be asking some rather leading questions in relation to finances and will need to get to the bottom of issues that have caused you some small problems in the past. The weekend also offers positive trends socially, with the possibility of a meeting of minds with someone very important.

5 SUNDAY
Moon Age Day 22 • Moon Sign Leo

am ....

pm ....

Sunday should offer you the chance to relax and take things more steadily than has been the case in the recent past. For some Librans, the pressures of the last week have been fairly intense and now you need some space to breathe. Try something completely different to brighten the day.

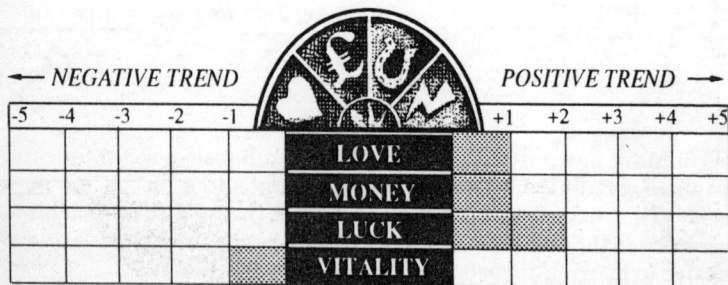

← *NEGATIVE TREND*　　　　　　　　　*POSITIVE TREND* →

-5	-4	-3	-2	-1		+1	+2	+3	+4	+5
					LOVE					
					MONEY					
					LUCK					
					VITALITY					

YOUR MONTH AT A GLANCE

The twelve numbered boxes represent the important areas in your life. The key to the numbers you will find beneath the panel. A Sun above the number indicates that opportunities are around. A Cloud below the number, that you should be a bit defensive. Nothing above or below and life will be pretty ordinary.

1	2	3	4	5	6	7	8	9	10	11	12

KEY

1 Strength of Personality	7 One to One Relationships
2 Personal Finance	8 Questioning, Thinking & Deciding
3 Useful Information Gathering	9 External Influences / Education
4 Domestic Affairs	10 Career Aspirations
5 Pleasure & Romance	11 Teamwork Activities
6 Effective Work & Health	12 Unconscious Impulses

DECEMBER HIGHS AND LOWS

Here, I show how the rhythm of the Moon will affect you this month. Like the tide, your energies and abilities will rise and fall with its pattern. When it is above the date line, go-for-it. When it is below the line you should be resting.

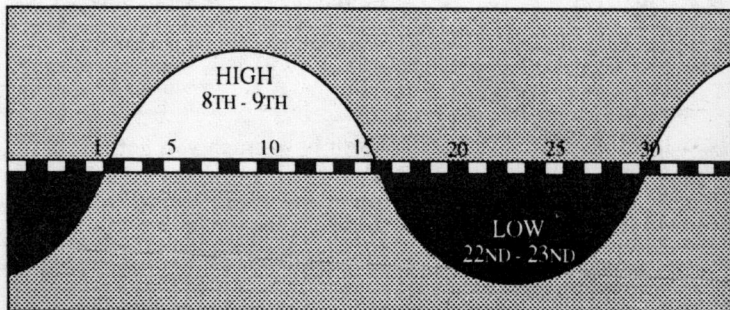

HIGH
8TH - 9TH

1   5   10   15   20   25   30

LOW
22ND - 23RD

6 MONDAY

Moon Age Day 23 • Moon Sign Virgo

am ....

pm ....

You may be doing all that you can to make your home surroundings as beautiful as possible now, and will also be looking out for the sort of people who take a reasoned and sensible view of life. Good news is on the way personally, with Librans in love especially joyful now.

7 TUESDAY

Moon Age Day 24 • Moon Sign Virgo

am ....

pm ....

As charming and persuasive as you always are at your best, there is little that you cannot get from other people now, simply by being in the right place and saying what your intuition tells you to be correct. Make certain that your own finances are safeguarded from the clutches of unscrupulous types, just for a day or two.

8 WEDNESDAY

Moon Age Day 25 • Moon Sign Libra

am ....

pm ....

The Moon now comes home to your sign, signifying the commencement of your lunar high for the month. You should be particularly persuasive with both employers and others who are in any sort of authority. This is a period when you should be able to turn almost any situation to your advantage.

9 THURSDAY

Moon Age Day 26 • Moon Sign Libra

am ....

pm ....

Life is flowing your way now, though how much you get out of it is partly down to the way that you are willing to go with the flow. Romantic attachments should begin to look especially rewarding and you can win all sorts of favours from a host of individuals, some of whom are strangers.

10 FRIDAY
Moon Age Day 27 • Moon Sign Scorpio

am ....

pm ....

Although you are presently full of energy, it would still be advisable to avoid taking on more than you really have to because the pendulum of life can all too easily turn back in the opposite direction, bringing fatigue and stress. Family news is apt to be quite cheering at present.

11 SATURDAY
Moon Age Day 28 • Moon Sign Scorpio

am ....

pm ....

Saturday brings a busy time, with social arrangements high on your agenda and plans for travel or meetings subject to last-minute revision. Be as straight as you can in all your dealings with other people, since much of what you have to say could all too easily be misconstrued at present.

12 SUNDAY
Moon Age Day 29 • Moon Sign Sagittarius

am ....

pm ....

Your only likely problem at present is a tendency to be too idealistic for your own good. The way ahead in life generally should be fairly smooth and you are not likely to be held back by much. All the same, you could be in need of more rest than you are getting now.

← *NEGATIVE TREND*   *POSITIVE TREND* →

-5	-4	-3	-2	-1		+1	+2	+3	+4	+5
					LOVE					
					MONEY					
					LUCK					
					VITALITY					

13 MONDAY

Moon Age Day 0 • Moon Sign Sagittarius

am ....

pm ....

A good period for achieving progress in your career, or for acting in an advisory role when dealing with others. Romantically speaking, you are probably calmer than of late and more willing to look at things in a detached and sensible manner. It is a realistic Libran who makes decisions this week.

14 TUESDAY

Moon Age Day 1 • Moon Sign Sagittarius

am ....

pm ....

In a domestic sense there are problems to be dealt with, not that these should cause you any more than a little inconvenience at present. All practical matters look especially good, though more patience is required in your dealings with people who appear determined to rub you up the wrong way.

15 WEDNESDAY

Moon Age Day 2 • Moon Sign Capricorn

am ....

pm ....

Although there is a tendency to get yourself involved in some rather serious debates today, there is some doubt as to whether you should really be getting involved at all. It might be far better to simply wait and see what the latter part of the day brings, remaining calm in the interim.

16 THURSDAY

Moon Age Day 3 • Moon Sign Capricorn

am ....

pm ....

Romantic issues are very much to the forefront of your thinking at present, though the fact that you are also keeping one eye on a rapidly approaching festive season could distract you even from these considerations. Personal confidence could be a little low at first.

17 FRIDAY

Moon Age Day 4 • Moon Sign Aquarius

am ....

pm ....

Probably a little too serious for your own good today, some of the otherwise positive social prospects could be spoiled by a rather negative attitude on your part. Good advice certainly is not in short supply, though there is nothing to indicate that you are bound to be listening.

18 SATURDAY

Moon Age Day 5 • Moon Sign Aquarius

am ....

pm ....

This is a day when you may have to justify your actions in a number of ways, not least of all on the social scene, where you may be also accused of hogging the limelight. Perhaps other people are a little too sensitive for their own good, though it might be difficult to discover.

19 SUNDAY

Moon Age Day 6 • Moon Sign Pisces

am ....

pm ....

If there appears to be a lack of practical progress, now is the time to knuckle down and to decide how you can improve the situation. Although it could be somewhat difficult to deal with all routine matters at the weekend, situations in the planning stage should be subjected to close scrutiny.

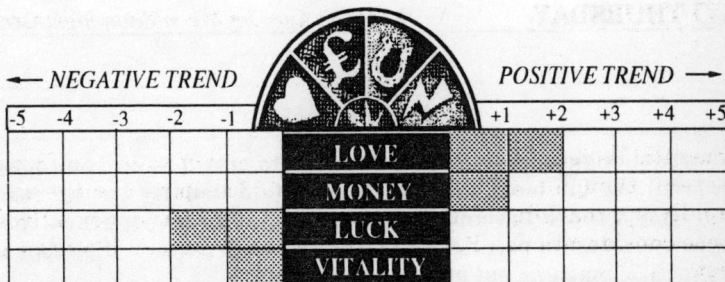

← *NEGATIVE TREND*   *POSITIVE TREND* →

-5	-4	-3	-2	-1		+1	+2	+3	+4	+5
					LOVE					
					MONEY					
					LUCK					
					VITALITY					

20 MONDAY
Moon Age Day 7 • Moon Sign Pisces

am ....

pm ....

Mars now enters your solar fourth house of home base matters, so you can expect a more dynamic phase to open up in this area. You may need to calm down one or two of the more exuberant family members, though it would be difficult to curb all the excitement that exists at this time of the year.

21 TUESDAY
Moon Age Day 8 • Moon Sign Pisces

am ....

pm ....

The lunar low beckons, and though you do not really begin to feel its influence fully until tomorrow, you will be slowing down in some practical matters and taking the time to think about actions. Not everyone that you meet at this stage is equally reliable, so exercise care.

22 WEDNESDAY
Moon Age Day 9 • Moon Sign Aries

am ....

pm ....

Not an ideal day to allow yourself to become dispirited, after all, there are many aspects of life that are going really well for you at present and all you really need is slightly more confidence in yourself when dealing with them. A good time for planning, though not for dynamic actions.

23 THURSDAY
Moon Age Day 10 • Moon Sign Aries

am ....

pm ....

Private thoughts and emotions are apt to crowd in on you today, making you far more pensive than would usually be the case. Familiar people are important to you at present, since they represent an air of normality that you can latch onto. Critics abound in practical matters, but are not significant.

24 FRIDAY

Moon Age Day 11 • Moon Sign Taurus

am ....

pm ....

Intimate relationships are inclined to fall under the spotlight today and you will be giving some thought to the needs of your partner on this Christmas Eve. A general feeling of excitement could be rather late arriving at your door this year, though it should be evident by this evening.

25 SATURDAY

Moon Age Day 12 • Moon Sign Taurus

am ....

pm ....

If you were thinking that Christmas Day would give you the chance to unwind and relax, think again. There won't be too many moments to spend in your own company, though it is unlikely that you will worry about that fact too much. You are able to feed off the excitement of everyone you encounter.

26 SUNDAY

Moon Age Day 13 • Moon Sign Taurus

am ....

pm ....

Look out for some domestic disagreements, even if you are not the one who is actually creating them. It should be possible to nip any problems in the bud, before they have the chance to get out of hand. Renewed confidence in your own abilities allows you to look at old plans in a new light.

← NEGATIVE TREND							POSITIVE TREND →				
-5	-4	-3	-2	-1			+1	+2	+3	+4	+5
					LOVE						
					MONEY						
					LUCK						
					VITALITY						

27 MONDAY
Moon Age Day 14 • Moon Sign Gemini

am ....

pm ....

As Venus enters your solar fourth house, you find a period opening up that is particularly good for all forms of entertaining at home. This should be a domestically harmonious interlude, with favours from loved ones and friends being the rule and not the exception. There should be more room to please yourself.

28 TUESDAY
Moon Age Day 15 • Moon Sign Gemini

am ....

pm ....

A high profile is likely now, though you will have to be careful that you do not allow sentiment to cloud your more practical judgements. There should be no lack of confidence and all leisure interests are looking good as the week advances. Some tiredness should be taken into account.

29 WEDNESDAY
Moon Age Day 16 • Moon Sign Cancer

am ....

pm ....

Look out for good news regarding all your personal plans and objectives. It is important that you consider your next moves in a practical sense very carefully. In your home life too there are likely to be one or two considerations that are worth a second look and a closer scrutiny.

30 THURSDAY
Moon Age Day 17 • Moon Sign Cancer

am ....

pm ....

Some impatience with minor responsibilities will have to be dealt with in a sensible and rational way today. The social trends are slowing a little, for even Libra can have too much of a good thing. Be careful that you do not upset loved ones with remarks that are ill-considered or tactless.

31 FRIDAY

Moon Age Day 18 • Moon Sign Leo

am ....

pm ....

There are many comings and goings in your everyday life now, with new friends appearing and old ones beginning to become less important. Take a sensible view of the months ahead and you will realise that life is working out pretty much as you would wish. Comfort is easy to find at present for Librans who are willing to look.

1 SATURDAY

Moon Age Day 19 • Moon Sign Leo

am ....

pm ....

Look out for some cause for concern regarding your love-life on the very first day of the new year. It does not appear that everyone is on your side just at present, though this is really no time to be making enemies. With a reasonable attitude all round, there is a chance to get back on good terms.

2 SUNDAY

Moon Age Day 20 • Moon Sign Virgo

am ....

pm ....

Emotional involvements bring some added spice to your life as situations generally begin to look far more rewarding than has been the case for a while. Even so, you can gain even more by concentrating on certain people, bringing them round to what you understand to be a more reasonable point of view.

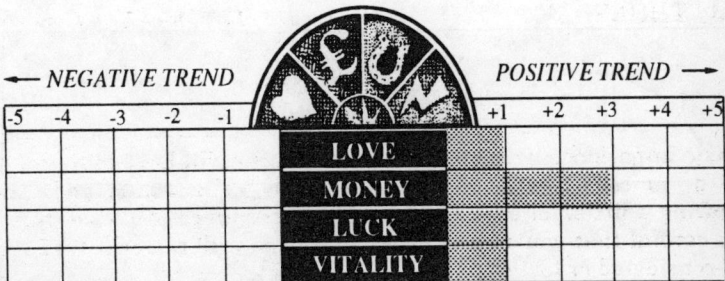

← NEGATIVE TREND						POSITIVE TREND →				
-5	-4	-3	-2	-1		+1	+2	+3	+4	+5
					LOVE					
					MONEY					
					LUCK					
					VITALITY					

1994

YOUR MONTH AT A GLANCE

The twelve numbered boxes represent the important areas in your life. The key to the numbers you will find beneath the panel. A Sun above the number indicates that opportunities are around. A Cloud below the number, that you should be a bit defensive. Nothing above or below and life will be pretty ordinary.

KEY

1 Strength of Personality	7 One to One Relationships
2 Personal Finance	8 Questioning, Thinking & Deciding
3 Useful Information Gathering	9 External Influences / Education
4 Domestic Affairs	10 Career Aspirations
5 Pleasure & Romance	11 Teamwork Activities
6 Effective Work & Health	12 Unconscious Impulses

JANUARY HIGHS AND LOWS

Here, I show how the rhythm of the Moon will affect you this month. Like the tide, your energies and abilities will rise and fall with its pattern. When it is above the date line, go-for-it. When it is below the line you should be resting.

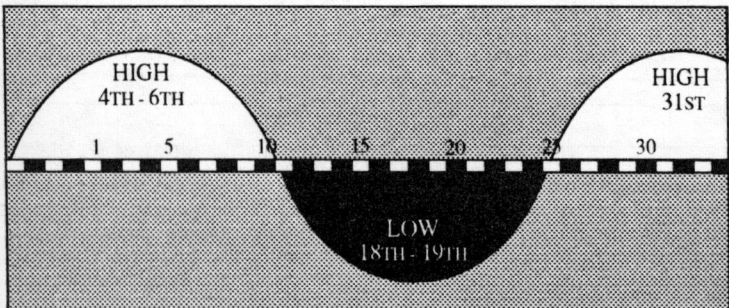

HIGH
4TH - 6TH

HIGH
31ST

LOW
18TH - 19TH

3 MONDAY

Moon Age Day 21 • Moon Sign Virgo

am ....

pm ....

Financial issues do not stand out as being very important, and in one way or another these can receive an added boost, courtesy of the attitude of loved ones. Friends too are very supportive at the moment, though in a more general way. You could do worse than to listen as they make much of your good points.

4 TUESDAY

Moon Age Day 22 • Moon Sign Libra

am ....

pm ....

Along comes the first lunar high of the New Year, that period of the month when the Moon occupies your own sign of Libra. This should put you in a very productive mood, and may enable you to make the sort of genuine progress that could have been lacking since before the holiday period. Now you are in full swing.

5 WEDNESDAY

Moon Age Day 23 • Moon Sign Libra

am ....

pm ....

What a day for being in the right place at the right time, and for making a great impact on the world around you. You should soon discover that you are on a winning streak, even if this does not show out immediately in hard financial terms. Confidence is supported by a very determined attitude from your direction.

6 THURSDAY

Moon Age Day 24 • Moon Sign Libra

am ....

pm ....

Stay on the lookout for new financial opportunities that should be on the way before very long. You can be naturally protective, both of yourself and on behalf of the people for whom you care deeply at the moment. What you can't afford to do is to try and wrap them up in cotton wool. In the end, their own choices are important too.

7 FRIDAY
Moon Age Day 25 • Moon Sign Scorpio

am ....

pm ....

A combination of Venus and Mars working on your behalf now makes you especially good in partnerships on one sort or another, and should make it possible for you to get on better with people who have not always seemed to be on your side in the past. You can contribute to what should be a happy period all round.

8 SATURDAY
Moon Age Day 26 • Moon Sign Scorpio

am ....

pm ....

Along comes the weekend, and it is the practicalities of life that demand your attention for the majority of the time. Take a close look at family finances and avoid the attitude that says, spend now, worry about it later. You have to keep a tight hold on money at present, and will be glad you did later.

9 SUNDAY
Moon Age Day 27 • Moon Sign Sagittarius

am ....

pm ....

On the move, with little time to collect your thoughts together, unless you are careful this could turn out to be one of the busiest Sundays of the month. Be willing to find a few moments to put your feet up, during which you should be able to please yourself. Friends contribute to a happy time personally later on.

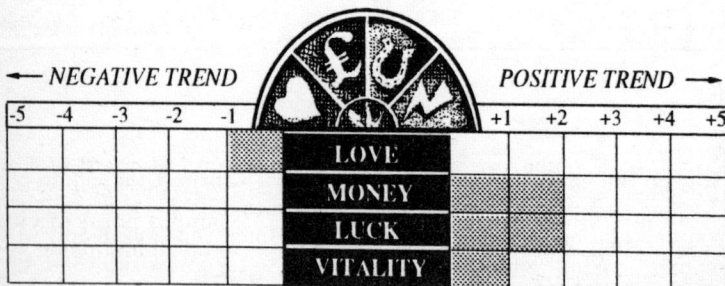

← NEGATIVE TREND							POSITIVE TREND →			
-5	-4	-3	-2	-1		+1	+2	+3	+4	+5
					LOVE					
					MONEY					
					LUCK					
					VITALITY					

10 MONDAY

Moon Age Day 28 • Moon Sign Sagittarius

am ....

pm ....

A period that stimulates your romantic imagination, with an aspect of the Sun and Neptune making you rather dreamy and quite sentimental. Emotionally speaking, this time should be quite rewarding, particularly since there are so many people who could have something good to say about you.

11 TUESDAY

Moon Age Day 29 • Moon Sign Capricorn

am ....

pm ....

There is much contentment to be had at present, simply from settling back and watching the way that life looks after itself. You certainly do not have to be running around at a fantastic speed today in order to make the sort of progress that you seek. In a personal relationship, a new understanding is on the way.

12 WEDNESDAY

Moon Age Day 0 • Moon Sign Capricorn

am ....

pm ....

Though an ability to handle your finances wisely and with commonsense still remains, it would be sensible all the same, not to take on more than you know is sensible in the way of fiscal responsibility at present. An attitude of easy come easy go now will only lead to some real problems further down the line.

13 THURSDAY

Moon Age Day 1 • Moon Sign Aquarius

am ....

pm ....

Around your home you should find an area of excitement and significant potential. thanks to the presence of Mercury, now in your solar fourth house. However, from a professional point of view, there is little doubt that superiors make greater demands on you, which may not exactly please you at the moment.

14 FRIDAY

Moon Age Day 2 • Moon Sign Aquarius

am ....

pm ....

Look out for some especially rewarding encounters, no matter if they relate to people who you know well, or perhaps total strangers. Light relief from the routines of your working life are now in the offing, the more so because you see the weekend as a period for being yourself. Plan now for the next couple of days.

15 SATURDAY

Moon Age Day 3 • Moon Sign Pisces

am ....

pm ....

Family members contribute to a generally settled and happy time for you today, though in one way or another you will still have things on your mind that cannot be dealt with via close relationships. Not a day for thinking too much however, and much more the type of period to let things ride a little.

16 SUNDAY

Moon Age Day 4 • Moon Sign Pisces

am ....

pm ....

Help and co-operation are the hallmarks of the day. If you work at the weekend, this comes via your professional life, whilst for those Librans who are at home, it is towards family members that new understanding is being turned. You can easily see a point of view that is not the same as your own.

← *NEGATIVE TREND*   *POSITIVE TREND* →

-5	-4	-3	-2	-1			+1	+2	+3	+4	+5
					LOVE						
					MONEY						
					LUCK						
					VITALITY						

17 MONDAY

Moon Age Day 5 • Moon Sign Pisces

am ....

pm ....

This would not be exactly the best time to try and make things happen in a career sense, all the more reason to take a look at what life has to offer in other ways. Confidence to do what seems right from a personal standpoint is not far from you, though even here you will have to be tactful and explain yourself.

18 TUESDAY

Moon Age Day 6 • Moon Sign Aries

am ....

pm ....

Energy can be low with the arrival of the lunar low, and though this is not a situation that will last for more than a couple of days, it can take the wind out of your sails a little. Perhaps you are in need of some rest in any case. Ignore the attitude problems of people you have to deal with at work.

19 WEDNESDAY

Moon Age Day 7 • Moon Sign Aries

am ....

pm ....

Sort out minor difficulties on your own. By the time you have got round to looking for the right person to consult, you could find that the advice on offer is not really practical for you. Later on you can benefit from the kindness of those in your vicinity, and from new romantic incentives that are created by your positive attitude.

20 THURSDAY

Moon Age Day 8 • Moon Sign Taurus

am ....

pm ....

Minor improvements are the order of the day, both in a professional and a personal sense. All the same, you will not be trying to move mountains at present and should take the possibilities of the day at face value. An interesting time with regard to hobbies or interests outside of your professional life.

21 FRIDAY
Moon Age Day 9 • Moon Sign Taurus

am ....

pm ....

Personal pleasure rises in importance as the Sun enters your solar fifth house. Romance can be important for the next month or so and there are new possibilities relating to the love lives of so many Librans just at present. It ought to be possible to let go and really be yourself for once, no matter what others think.

22 SATURDAY
Moon Age Day 10 • Moon Sign Taurus

am ....

pm ....

An excellent time for short breaks and pleasure trips of any sort. If the practicalities of everyday life, or money considerations, prevent you from getting out of the house too much, you could always settle down with a really good book. Your imagination now makes even this as good as a holiday in your mind.

23 SUNDAY
Moon Age Day 11 • Moon Sign Gemini

am ....

pm ....

Added spice comes to the more romantic side of your nature, mainly thanks to the position of Venus in your solar fifth house. Someone could be showing a great deal on interest in you, and at a time when you haven't been especially high in your own estimation. A generally rewarding and interesting period.

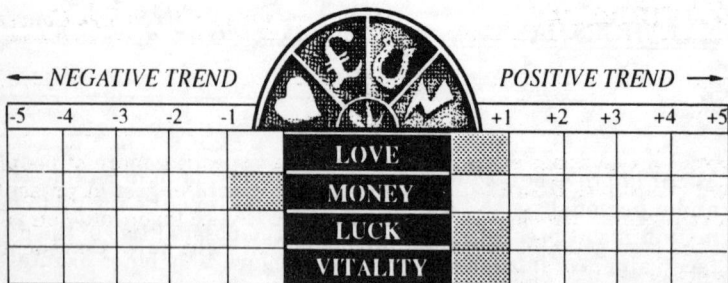

← NEGATIVE TREND								POSITIVE TREND →			
-5	-4	-3	-2	-1			+1	+2	+3	+4	+5
					LOVE						
					MONEY						
					LUCK						
					VITALITY						

24 MONDAY

Moon Age Day 12 • Moon Sign Gemini

am ....

pm ....

If you have been looking to make improvements to property, or to aspects of your life that could be considered of a practical nature, look no further than this time. Domestic alterations are undertaken in a spirit of real excitement, and for the first time this year you will have one eye focussed on the Spring.

25 TUESDAY

Moon Age Day 13 • Moon Sign Cancer

am ....

pm ....

Tricky issues personally are soon dealt with, even if certain people around you are doing their best to be difficult. In conversation you are supreme, which is why you could easily find yourself to be the centre of attraction from a social point-of-view. Even casual conversations have something to offer.

26 WEDNESDAY

Moon Age Day 14 • Moon Sign Cancer

am ....

pm ....

You definitely need to get your priorities right at present, especially since not everyone is in the right mood to help you out. Loved ones could seem to have a rather heavy attitude to life and will need the sort of gentle support that you are so good at offering. Your own diplomacy is the best guarantee of success for a few days.

27 THURSDAY

Moon Age Day 15 • Moon Sign Cancer

am ....

pm ....

Social happenings show that you may be expecting more of people and situations than they are willing or able to offer just at present. A reliance on people who have not always looked favourably on you in the past could be the worst mistake of all right now. Confidence is not especially high.

28 FRIDAY
Moon Age Day 16 • Moon Sign Leo

am ....

pm ....

Renewed high-spirits attend your life as Mars enters your solar fifth house, joining other planets presently there and contributing to a spirit of optimism as the month nears its end. You are the person who takes the lead in organising the fun and games in your own life, encouraging others on the way.

29 SATURDAY
Moon Age Day 17 • Moon Sign Leo

am ....

pm ....

Although the weekend may actively prevent you from doing anything about it, you should find that your mind is turning very much in the direction of professional matters today. This would be a good time to do some planning, though is less well-starred when it comes to putting your plans into action.

30 SUNDAY
Moon Age Day 18 • Moon Sign Virgo

am ....

pm ....

You have to bear the feeling of others in mind, even on those occasions when you really don't see their point of view. In one way or another this could make today a little complicated, particularly since people in your vicinity could be especially prickly at present. Make the most of all new social encounters.

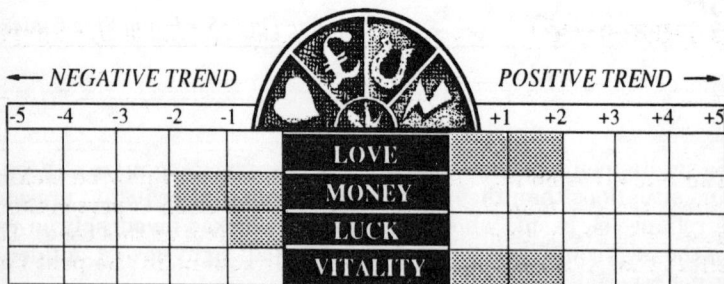

← NEGATIVE TREND						POSITIVE TREND →				
-5	-4	-3	-2	-1		+1	+2	+3	+4	+5
					LOVE					
					MONEY					
					LUCK					
					VITALITY					

31 MONDAY

Moon Age Day 19 • Moon Sign Virgo

am ....

pm ....

The lunar high brings along a feeling that you can do almost anything. Take some decisive action now and you will be pleased that you did so in the fullness of time. Romantic encounters are especially favourable, with friends also willing to help you out when they think that a little effort is advisable.

1 TUESDAY

Moon Age Day 20 • Moon Sign Libra

am ....

pm ....

Discussions and negotiations take on a more favourable aspect, and there is the chance to overcome shortcomings later in the day. The progress of life now looks smoother and there are less complications attending your life than would have been the case formerly. Offer your timely assistance to others.

2 WEDNESDAY

Moon Age Day 21 • Moon Sign Libra

am ....

pm ....

Although the present position of Mars is inclined to make you want your own way most of the time, be prepared to give a little ground on occasions. Compromise is essential, even though you may not exhibit a 'live and let live' attitude all of the day. Look to solving past problems mainly by being reasonable.

3 THURSDAY

Moon Age Day 22 • Moon Sign Scorpio

am ....

pm ....

There is a possibility that personal finances will now be looking much stronger than they have for a while. A clash of personalities at work is likely, though not particularly helpful at this time. The effort that you have put into several directions in the past now begins to work to your advantage.

4 FRIDAY
Moon Age Day 23 • Moon Sign Scorpio

am ....

pm ....

Make arrangements for travel today if you can, even where the actual journey could be weeks or even months in the future. Other people may expect you to settle for second best in major issues, though you are quite adamant about what you want from life right now. Confrontations should be avoided all the same.

5 SATURDAY
Moon Age Day 24 • Moon Sign Sagittarius

am ....

pm ....

The sympathy that you naturally show to others is aroused all to easily right now. As long as the recipients appreciate the fact and do not try to take advantage of it, then all should be well. Keep your eyes open though, because you could all too easily find yourself being duped at the present time.

6 SUNDAY
Moon Age Day 25 • Moon Sign Sagittarius

am ....

pm ....

Now the tables are turned and it is others who do their best to be of use to you. Even here you may sense that there are strings attached, and in any case there is much to be said for spending at least part of the day on your own. Do listen though because there is an attractive sounding proposition in the offing.

←— *NEGATIVE TREND*   *POSITIVE TREND* —→

-5	-4	-3	-2	-1		+1	+2	+3	+4	+5
					LOVE					
					MONEY					
					LUCK					
					VITALITY					

1994

YOUR MONTH AT A GLANCE

The twelve numbered boxes represent the important areas in your life. The key to the numbers you will find beneath the panel. A Sun above the number indicates that opportunities are around. A Cloud below the number, that you should be a bit defensive. Nothing above or below and life will be pretty ordinary.

1	2	3	4	5	6	7	8	9	10	11	12

KEY

1 Strength of Personality
2 Personal Finance
3 Useful Information Gathering
4 Domestic Affairs
5 Pleasure & Romance
6 Effective Work & Health

7 One to One Relationships
8 Questioning, Thinking & Deciding
9 External Influences / Education
10 Career Aspirations
11 Teamwork Activities
12 Unconscious Impulses

FEBRUARY HIGHS AND LOWS

Here, I show how the rhythm of the Moon will affect you this month. Like the tide, your energies and abilities will rise and fall with its pattern. When it is above the date line, go-for-it. When it is below the line you should be resting.

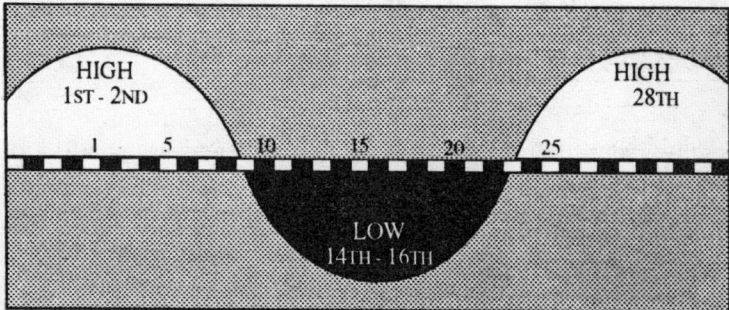

HIGH
1ST - 2ND

HIGH
28TH

1   5   10   15   20   25

LOW
14TH - 16TH

7 MONDAY
Moon Age Day 26 • Moon Sign Capricorn

am ....

pm ....

Domestic responsibilities can clash with your plans in other directions, which is why you should do all that you can to make the most out of situations, though without trying to spread yourself too thinly. Don't be too critical of others, especially since they could be of great use to you in a personal sense.

8 TUESDAY
Moon Age Day 27 • Moon Sign Capricorn

am ....

pm ....

The emphasis for today is upon matters close to hearth and home. Even if you work during the day, you should find your mind returning to domestic possibilities and you can make the most of any free time in the company of those you live with. A sense of proportion is all-important however, and worry is definitely out.

9 WEDNESDAY
Moon Age Day 28 • Moon Sign Aquarius

am ....

pm ....

Although there is still some excitement about in certain areas of your life, you should find that things are calming down significantly. Certain people, and probably your partner, appear to be taking life far more seriously than you might think is good for them. Turn on the charm and cheer them up if you can.

10 THURSDAY
Moon Age Day 0 • Moon Sign Aquarius

am ....

pm ....

It would be all too easy now to try and please everyone all of the time. An element of competition enters your life and makes it essential that you are out in the mainstream of events, happy to do what you can to help others, but also anxious to feather your own nest when the opportunity arises.

11 FRIDAY

Moon Age Day 1 • Moon Sign Aquarius

am ....

pm ....

Not everyone is impressed with either your ideas or your behaviour at the present time. All the more reason to put in that extra bit of effort to show them that you mean business. Progress could never be as fast at present as you might wish it to be, but that does not mean that life is standing still.

12 SATURDAY

Moon Age Day 2 • Moon Sign Pisces

am ....

pm ....

Now you can accomplish far more, or is it just that the effort you have put in during the last few days is at last paying off? Be aware that much of your optimism, although laudable, may be somewhat premature. A slow and steady approach to situations may suit you the best of all, and some time to do what you really want.

13 SUNDAY

Moon Age Day 3 • Moon Sign Pisces

am ....

pm ....

Venus enters your solar sixth house, placing the accent firmly upon getting things done and feeling more satisfied with specific aspects of your life. This position of Venus can also encourage the more luxury-loving qualities of your nature, and could encourage you to spend more than would be really sensible.

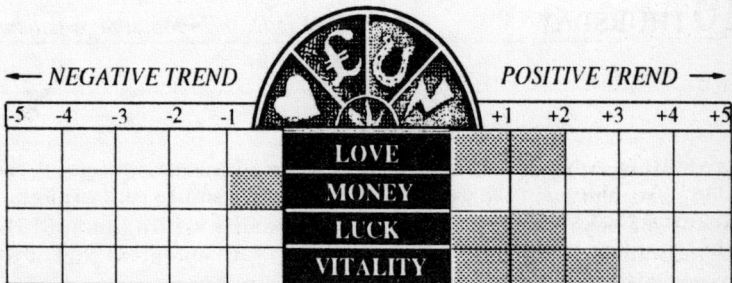

← *NEGATIVE TREND*   *POSITIVE TREND* →

-5	-4	-3	-2	-1			+1	+2	+3	+4	+5
					LOVE						
					MONEY						
					LUCK						
					VITALITY						

14 MONDAY
Moon Age Day 4 • Moon Sign Aries

am ....

pm ....

Because the lunar low places the Moon in the zodiac sign opposite your own, you really can't hope to make the sort of general progress that you may be looking for. It is easy enough for Libra to be patient, though perhaps less so at present. Too much reliance on others is not what you will be looking for.

15 TUESDAY
Moon Age Day 5 • Moon Sign Aries

am ....

pm ....

Keep the lid on your ambitions, at least until tomorrow, for this is not an ideal period to try and get new plans off the ground. Friends can disappoint you with their attitudes, but can be of real assistance when it comes to the more practical aspects of life. It is practicality that you are searching for yourself.

16 WEDNESDAY
Moon Age Day 6 • Moon Sign Aries

am ....

pm ....

Mars strong in your solar fifth house, emphasises the need you have of help and support from people you recognise as being very fixed in character. For your own part, it would be quite easy to scatter your energy in the days ahead, even though there is no doubt that you have much to offer the world.

17 THURSDAY
Moon Age Day 7 • Moon Sign Taurus

am ....

pm ....

With others now so willing to confide their innermost secrets, you won't be surprised to discover that today turns out to be an emotional sort of day. In your own way you are also willing to spill the beans a little, with feelings of warmth being an operative part of the scenario, even to people who are only acquaintances.

18 FRIDAY

Moon Age Day 8 • Moon Sign Taurus

am ....

pm ....

There are certainly some obstacles about today when it comes to making the sort of changes that you see as being quite essential. However, this does not mean that you lack any kind of influence, so in almost any situation it is still worth having a go. Remain determined, even if there are some obstacles about.

19 SATURDAY

Moon Age Day 9 • Moon Sign Gemini

am ....

pm ....

The Sun enters your solar sixth house, bringing you to a time when you should notice more support from a practical point of view. The past effort that you have put in now begins to show in terms of hard, practical rewards. Not everyone is exactly helpful at present, though with effort you can make people change their tune.

20 SUNDAY

Moon Age Day 10 • Moon Sign Gemini

am ....

pm ....

Distractions are all too likely today, since it is not easy to keep your mind focussed in a particular direction. Be careful to finish what you have started in any sphere of your life, leaving at least a little time to show your partner and those who are close to you exactly how much you care for them.

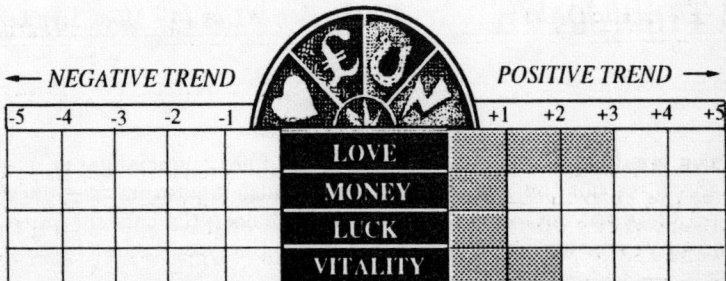

← NEGATIVE TREND								POSITIVE TREND →				
-5	-4	-3	-2	-1			+1	+2	+3	+4	+5
					LOVE						
					MONEY						
					LUCK						
					VITALITY						

21 MONDAY
Moon Age Day 11 • Moon Sign Gemini

am ....

pm ....

Getting other people to make a decision will not be at all easy today, which is why you find you are getting the impression that they are stalling for time. You can't really force issues without giving offence and so it might be best just to wait and see what happens. Stick to a rational point-of-view.

22 TUESDAY
Moon Age Day 12 • Moon Sign Cancer

am ....

pm ....

Romantic issues can be very important today, though in some ways a little unclear. Pinning your hopes entirely on social or personal matters could lead to a little disappointment now, which is why you should be taking a broad over view of life if this proves to be at all possible to do. In all areas, try to get at the truth.

23 WEDNESDAY
Moon Age Day 13 • Moon Sign Cancer

am ....

pm ....

Pulling together with your friends now seems to be more productive and far less problematic than it has been for quite a number of days. In some ways this is especially important at present, since you are not likely to achieve entirely on the grounds of your own effort. Co-operations can work wonders though.

24 THURSDAY
Moon Age Day 14 • Moon Sign Leo

am ....

pm ....

A combination of Venus and Jupiter now offers financial gains, even if these are not obvious at first. It could also mean that friends are even more willing to lend a hand than has been the case for quite a while. A greater sense of security is the likely outcome of today's events, both personally and professionally.

25 FRIDAY

Moon Age Day 15 • Moon Sign Leo

am ....

pm ....

Although it could seem that others are holding you back in some way, in reality you have rarely been more in command of your own destiny than is the case just at present. Domestically speaking, you may not be quite as settled as you wish, though arguments within the family are probably no more than a storm in a teacup.

26 SATURDAY

Moon Age Day 16 • Moon Sign Virgo

am ....

pm ....

Personal matters threaten to distract you from the more practical aspects of life, though certainly not for long. Make the most of having a strong social aspect to your life at present by being in the right place at the right time. You could show a tendency to allow your imagination to run riot more than is good for you.

27 SUNDAY

Moon Age Day 17 • Moon Sign Virgo

am ....

pm ....

With the lunar high now surrounding you, you should be on the lookout for significant help coming from the direction of both loved ones and friends. Now is the time to get out there and to ask for what you really want. Some influential types can be of great assistance, assuming that you have the courage to ask.

← NEGATIVE TREND							POSITIVE TREND →			
-5	-4	-3	-2	-1		+1	+2	+3	+4	+5
					LOVE	▓	▓			
				▓	MONEY					
			▓	▓	LUCK					
					VITALITY	▓	▓	▓		

28 MONDAY
Moon Age Day 18 • Moon Sign Libra

am ....

pm ....

The start of the new working week coincides with the surge of power that runs through you at present, allowing a very positive attitude and plenty of determination just when you need it the most. Don't pass up any opportunity to please yourself or to come to terms with those who are in the same mood as you are.

1 TUESDAY
Moon Age Day 19 • Moon Sign Libra

am ....

pm ....

Able to organise the practical aspects of your life in a sensible and rational manner, you approach all situations with a mixture of intuition and action. Friends are very helpful, even concerning situations that may have found them less than willing in the past. Utilise tried and tested paths of progress.

2 WEDNESDAY
Moon Age Day 20 • Moon Sign Scorpio

am ....

pm ....

Now you turn most of your attention back in the direction of your home, even though there is still plenty in the outside world to occupy your mind too. Friends may be in need of the sort of reassurance that you excel at offering. Patience is called into play regarding more personal aspects of your life.

3 THURSDAY
Moon Age Day 21 • Moon Sign Scorpio

am ....

pm ....

Financial delays mean having to be patient concerning personal acquisitions, not a situation that should worry you too much just at the present time. If you feel in some ways that you are kicking your heels, you may decide that the time is right for some new type of adventure to lift your spirits.

4 FRIDAY
Moon Age Day 22 • Moon Sign Sagittarius

am ....

pm ....

Meetings with others can bring a slight difference of opinion, but you should avoid allowing yourself to take these too seriously just at present. Don't let others pressure you into taking steps that are not really what you want. The influence of people in your vicinity cannot be over-stressed for the moment.

5 SATURDAY
Moon Age Day 23 • Moon Sign Sagittarius

am ....

pm ....

The emphasis now should be upon having fun and doing everything in your own special way. Make the most of what the days ahead have to offer from a personal point of view and avoid taking any situation more seriously than you have to. It's a 'never a dull moment' sort of interlude, and one that you can really appreciate.

6 SUNDAY
Moon Age Day 24 • Moon Sign Capricorn

am ....

pm ....

With an ability to set matters straight, you should now be able to come to terms with situations from the past that have been really difficult. You see almost everything in a clear and concise way just now, offering an unfettered view of the world and the incredible diversity of people inhabiting it.

← *NEGATIVE TREND*   *POSITIVE TREND* →

-5	-4	-3	-2	-1		+1	+2	+3	+4	+5
					LOVE					
					MONEY					
					LUCK					
					VITALITY					

1994

YOUR MONTH AT A GLANCE

The twelve numbered boxes represent the important areas in your life. The key to the numbers you will find beneath the panel. A Sun above the number indicates that opportunities are around. A Cloud below the number, that you should be a bit defensive. Nothing above or below and life will be pretty ordinary.

☀	☀									☀	
1	2	3	4	5	6	7	8	9	10	11	12
									☁		☁

KEY	
1 Strength of Personality	7 One to One Relationships
2 Personal Finance	8 Questioning, Thinking & Deciding
3 Useful Information Gathering	9 External Influences / Education
4 Domestic Affairs	10 Career Aspirations
5 Pleasure & Romance	11 Teamwork Activities
6 Effective Work & Health	12 Unconscious Impulses

MARCH HIGHS AND LOWS

Here, I show how the rhythm of the Moon will affect you this month. Like the tide, your energies and abilities will rise and fall with its pattern. When it is above the date line, go-for-it. When it is below the line you should be resting.

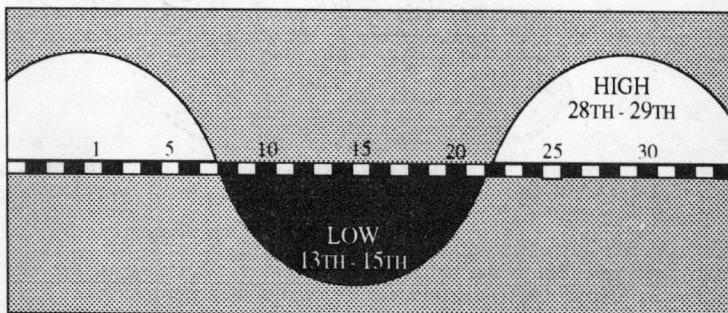

HIGH
28TH - 29TH

1   5   10   15   20   25   30

LOW
13TH - 15TH

7 MONDAY
Moon Age Day 25 • Moon Sign Capricorn

am ....

pm ....

People seem to want to push you along today, not that you will be able to go any faster than is sensible in anything. Through it all you remain your patient and easy-going self, which if nothing else should bring everyone round to your way of thinking in the end. Socially, the day should be good.

8 TUESDAY
Moon Age Day 26 • Moon Sign Capricorn

am ....

pm ....

Pressure eases in your life generally, so that the laid-back approach settles in for a day or two. You can make an especially good impression on almost anyone you meet right now and should be able to keep up with what is expected of you, at the same time planning carefully for the future.

9 WEDNESDAY
Moon Age Day 27 • Moon Sign Aquarius

am ....

pm ....

Venus now enters your solar seventh house and it seems as though everyone has your best interests at heart. For most Librans there are good associations to come personally, with the single amongst you on the receiving end of requests and invitations. An interlude to go out and get what you want from relationships.

10 THURSDAY
Moon Age Day 28• Moon Sign Aquarius

am ....

pm ....

Take life one project at a time today. In some respects the ideas do not flow quite as well at present and that means being more considered and utilising your intuition to a greater degree. Some enthusiasm could be lacking, though don't assume that there is a slow-down on the way, merely a quiet interlude.

11 FRIDAY
Moon Age Day 29 • Moon Sign Pisces

am ....

pm ....

With a greater clarity coming to your thinking, personal associations especially look really good now. Not only will your partner have some kind words for you, but you are able to express yourself well too. Most children of Venus should find this to be a high-spirited and relaxed time, with optimism abounding.

12 SATURDAY
Moon Age Day 0 • Moon Sign Pisces

am ....

pm ....

Once you have made up your mind about almost anything, you should be willing to act upon it. Although the weekend offers a new set of possibilities, your mind could still be running over all the associations from earlier days. It is doubtful if your attitude towards them will change significantly.

13 SUNDAY
Moon Age Day 1 • Moon Sign Aries

am ....

pm ....

You can expect a temporary lull today. The lunar low more or less forces a quiet spell into you life, though looking back across the last few days, it's doubtful that you will resist the urge to take things more steadily now. Try to spend at least a little time with family and friends, away from routines.

← *NEGATIVE TREND*   *POSITIVE TREND* →

	-5	-4	-3	-2	-1		+1	+2	+3	+4	+5
LOVE											
MONEY											
LUCK											
VITALITY											

14 MONDAY
Moon Age Day 2 • Moon Sign Aries

am ....

pm ....

With finances now less strong than you might wish and decisions taking an age to mature, what can you do except sit back and watch for a few hours? This will not do you any harm and could even fund a number of possibilities that are only in the early planning stage right now. Social possibilities beckon.

15 TUESDAY
Moon Age Day 3 • Moon Sign Aries

am ....

pm ....

Today you are able to take more interest again and the things that others have to say, even though many of them are simply casual remarks, will not fail to interest you a great deal. Self-determination is evident in most spheres of your life, though it could still be a little soon to be moving large mountains.

16 WEDNESDAY
Moon Age Day 4 • Moon Sign Taurus

am ....

pm ....

Original and even ingenious ideas are the possible gift of a favourable contact between the Sun and the planet Uranus. You could hardly be considered to be conventional in your approach to life for a day or two, a fact that makes you even more interesting to the people you live and work with.

17 THURSDAY
Moon Age Day 5 • Moon Sign Taurus

am ....

pm ....

Although there are now fluctuations in money matters, there is no doubt that you are making some real progress. The short-term is not ideal, so safeguard your interests if you can. Dramatic occurrences occupy the fringes of your life, though one or two fairly important facts come to light regarding your love-life.

18 FRIDAY

Moon Age Day 6 • Moon Sign Taurus

am ....

pm ....

Although you are very likely to be speaking your mind at the moment, there is always the possibility that you will say more than you really should in social situations. It's true that you have the best of intentions, but are others aware of the fact? Perhaps you should make your sympathy clear.

19 SATURDAY

Moon Age Day 7 • Moon Sign Gemini

am ....

pm ....

Despite the fact that you may feel like a change of scene with the weekend upon you, the fact is that you are tied in some way to the practical issues of the day. Friends and loved ones offer you some interesting alternatives, no matter how busy you may be. Don't turn them down out of hand.

20 SUNDAY

Moon Age Day 8 • Moon Sign Gemini

am ....

pm ....

Don't be surprised to find that people are chasing your attention personally. Meanwhile, you could well wake up to the fact that Spring is just around the corner, no matter what the weather is doing today. The thought can do much to inspire new domestic plans, and could even send you rushing off to the DIY shops.

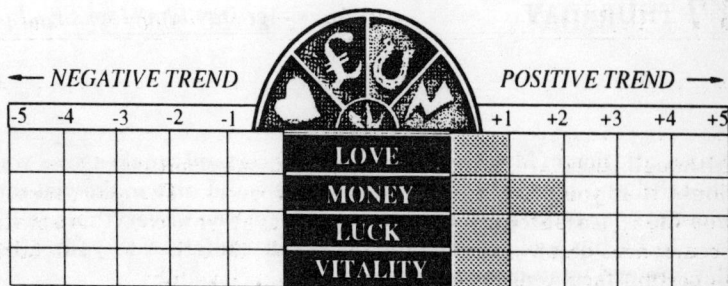

◄— NEGATIVE TREND　　　　　　　*POSITIVE TREND —►*

	-5	-4	-3	-2	-1		+1	+2	+3	+4	+5
LOVE											
MONEY											
LUCK											
VITALITY											

21 MONDAY
Moon Age Day 9 • Moon Sign Cancer

am ....

pm ....

Long-term planning becomes essential at the start of a new week. You need to be as realistic as possible when it comes to considering where you are going in life and should not be too willing to accept second best in anything. The week is potentially very progressive, though much depends on your attitude.

22 TUESDAY
Moon Age Day 10 • Moon Sign Cancer

am ....

pm ....

The Sun now enters your solar seventh house, stimulating a need for company and for social possibilities that remains strong for the next month or so. New friendships are in the offing, a situation that could start almost immediately. There is also the chance today to catch up with people from the past.

23 WEDNESDAY
Moon Age Day 11 • Moon Sign Leo

am ....

pm ....

Assistance comes just when you need it the most, and especially so if you are willing to keep your options open, refusing to dismiss any possibility out of hand. The things that you say to others can stimulate a few very interesting discussions and some of them could be associated with early travel-plans.

24 THURSDAY
Moon Age Day 12 • Moon Sign Leo

am ....

pm ....

An association of Mars and Jupiter today certainly makes for a very cheerful and quite dynamic Libran, but could also make you into more of a spendthrift than is really good for you. Everything in life has to be big and flashy now, as a contradiction to your often demure and unassuming nature.

25 FRIDAY

Moon Age Day 13 • Moon Sign Leo

am ....

pm ....

Compliments come from the direction of loved ones and friends alike. Partnerships of all kinds can now work in your favour. What is more extraordinary about today is the way that you play down your own abilities, in favour of highlighting those of the people in your vicinity.

26 SATURDAY

Moon Age Day 14 • Moon Sign Virgo

am ....

pm ....

With the Moon now entering the solar twelfth house of your chart, you should not be especially surprised to find that you become quieter and a little more withdrawn for today. It is the hustle and bustle of everyday life that you want to get away from for a few hours, even though to do so may not be especially easy.

27 SUNDAY

Moon Age Day 15 • Moon SignVirgo

am ....

pm ....

The Moon now moves into your own sign of Libra, probably offering one of the best Sundays potentially this year. It isn't that anything remarkable is likely to happen, merely that you are quite happy with the way that things are going generally. Friends and relatives alike choose to be helpful.

← *NEGATIVE TREND*								*POSITIVE TREND* →			
-5	-4	-3	-2	-1		+1	+2	+3	+4	+5
					LOVE					
					MONEY					
					LUCK					
					VITALITY					

28 MONDAY
Moon Age Day 16 • Moon Sign Libra

am ....

pm ....

It should not be too hard to bring others round to your way of thinking at the start of another busy and productive week. Important negotiations can take place in an air of genuine co-operation today. Bringing out the best in co-workers or people who are new on the scene is something you excel at right now.

29 TUESDAY
Moon Age Day 17 • Moon Sign Libra

am ....

pm ....

The behaviour of friends and family members alike could seem to be fairly erratic today, all the more reason to give them a little more room to think things out for themselves. What you can't really afford to do today is to relax into situations too much, but don't assume you are responsible for the world either.

30 WEDNESDAY
Moon Age Day 18 • Moon Sign Scorpio

am ....

pm ....

Present plans of action will have to be revised if you are to stand any hope of getting what you really want out of life in the middle of this particular week. Still, it isn't hard for Librans to adapt to changing circumstances and you could never be accused of being fixed in your opinions. A change of scene might help.

31 THURSDAY
Moon Age Day 19 • Moon Sign Scorpio

am ....

pm ....

Meetings and appointments could turn out to be only moderately successful for the moment, though this is no reason at all to allow negative thinking into your life. What you really need is the kind of boost that comes from attentive friends, and also from the people who support your ideas at work.

1 FRIDAY
Moon Age Day 20 • Moon Sign Sagittarius

am ....

pm ....

Disagreements over the best way to get things done could well turn
out to be a complete waste of time, especially since you may already
have your own ideas on most topics at present. You are certainly
nobody's April Fool when it comes to making up your own mind, but
you could fall for one or two tricks all the same.

2 SATURDAY
Moon Age Day 21 • Moon Sign Sagittarius

am ....

pm ....

The financial interests of others could be of importance to you too
right now, though you don't want to be accused of being nosy and
will want to do all that you can to foster good relations all round.
Changes to routines are not too difficult to make and in most
situations you can approach life with a smile.

3 SUNDAY
Moon Age Day 22 • Moon Sign Capricorn

am ....

pm ....

With an excellent period for making changes at home now
contributing to a busy and quite interesting routine, there should
also be significant personal attention around to make you happy to
be alive, with your partner proving to be especially attentive and
the events of the day contributing to your peace of mind.

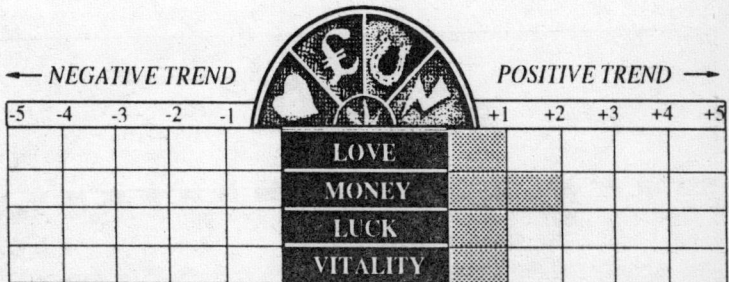

← *NEGATIVE TREND*									*POSITIVE TREND* →	
-5	-4	-3	-2	-1		+1	+2	+3	+4	+5
					LOVE					
					MONEY					
					LUCK					
					VITALITY					

1994
YOUR MONTH AT A GLANCE

The twelve numbered boxes represent the important areas in your life.
The key to the numbers you will find beneath the panel. A Sun above
the number indicates that opportunities are around. A Cloud below
the number, that you should be a bit defensive. Nothing above or
below and life will be pretty ordinary.

KEY

1 Strength of Personality
2 Personal Finance
3 Useful Information Gathering
4 Domestic Affairs
5 Pleasure & Romance
6 Effective Work & Health

7 One to One Relationships
8 Questioning, Thinking & Deciding
9 External Influences / Education
10 Career Aspirations
11 Teamwork Activities
12 Unconscious Impulses

APRIL HIGHS AND LOWS

Here, I show how the rhythm of the Moon will affect you this month.
Like the tide, your energies and abilities will rise and fall with its pattern. When it is above the date line, go-for-it. When it is below the
line you should be resting.

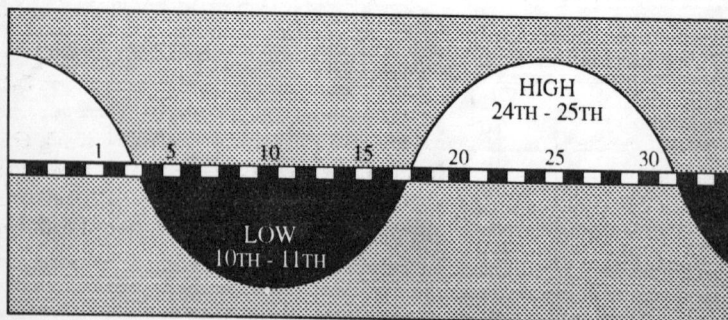

4 MONDAY
Moon Age Day 23 • Moon Sign Capricorn

am ....

pm ....

Romance is significant on the agenda for you at the start of this working week, and you should find that you are high in the popularity stakes generally. If there is a fly in the ointment at present it might be that you are a little too exuberant for your own good. Keep your options open in a professional sense.

5 TUESDAY
Moon Age Day 24 • Moon Sign Aquarius

am ....

pm ....

Any obligations that you feel towards others should be carried out in a spirit of genuine compromise and always with the best interests of your friends and relatives in your mind. The very best kind of Libran is in evidence today, so there is little wonder that you get positive reactions coming back at you.

6 WEDNESDAY
Moon Age Day 25 • Moon Sign Aquarius

am ....

pm ....

Although you are still more than willing to compromise, there is the slight danger that you may be bearing the other person's point of view in mind just a little more than you should. A positive boost to personal relationships of all kinds comes along now, probably lifting the latter part of the day no end.

7 THURSDAY
Moon Age Day 26 • Moon Sign Pisces

am ....

pm ....

Circumstances seem to pressure you into taking on more work than you might reasonably be expected to cope with now, which is why the advice of Old Moore is to make certain that you take at least some time out to be yourself. Confidences come from a number of different directions as the days advance.

8 FRIDAY
Moon Age Day 27 • Moon Sign Pisces

am ....

pm ....

Joint financial matters show some improvement, and allow you to discuss things fully with people who matter in your life. Invaluable advice comes from people who know both you and the way that you like to live your life. There are some very intuitive types about at present, and you have access to them.

9 SATURDAY
Moon Age Day 28 • Moon Sign Pisces

am ....

pm ....

Don't be too surprised if you lack a little drive and ambition today. The lunar low makes it rather difficult to make the sort of progress that you are looking for, though this does not mean that your life has come to a halt. On the contrary, today is excellent for leisure pursuits and for planning.

10 SUNDAY
Moon Age Day 29 • Moon Sign Aries

am ....

pm ....

Solutions now come along to problems that have been on your mind for quite some time. Your partner, or a close friend, can be especially helpful when it comes to practical decisions that have been waiting for some time. If the weather is kind, get out of doors for an hour or two at some stage.

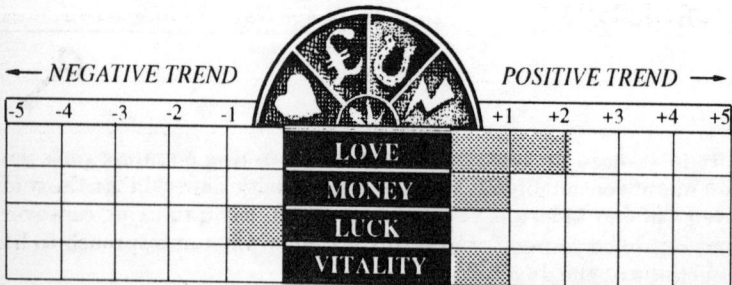

← *NEGATIVE TREND*   *POSITIVE TREND* →

-5	-4	-3	-2	-1			+1	+2	+3	+4	+5
					LOVE						
					MONEY						
					LUCK						
					VITALITY						

11 MONDAY

Moon Age Day 0 • Moon Sign Aries

am ....

pm ....

Although a new working week stands before you, there is a possibility that you lack some of the real drive necessary to make the sort of progress that you suspect to be lacking in your life at the moment. The Moon moves on later today, and almost immediately you will feel more determined and optimistic.

12 TUESDAY

Moon Age Day 1 • Moon Sign Taurus

am ....

pm ....

There are mixed influences regarding your working life today, though these should be more than compensated for by your general attitude, which leans more in the direction of personal and social possibilities. The moment that you are dealing with appears to be the only really important factor for now.

13 WEDNESDAY

Moon Age Day 2 • Moon Sign Taurus

am ....

pm ....

The effort you always manage to put in, even on those occasions when not everything is going your way, really begin to pay off now. The best feature of the day relates to the fact that almost everyone you encounter seems to be pulling their weight and should be willing to help you out in some way.

14 THURSDAY

Moon Age Day 3 • Moon Sign Taurus

am ....

pm ....

A slightly tenuous aspect between the Sun and Neptune puts you into a more dreamy mood than you might have expected for the middle of the week. Not that this is a particularly bad thing however, because it means that you are inspirational in your approach to life and become more so as the day jogs on.

15 FRIDAY
Moon Age Day 4 • Moon Sign Gemini

am ....

pm ....

Some restlessness in one-to-one relationships is best coped with by being willing to look at the wider spectrum of friendships. You will not find yourself relying on one person at all today, particularly since there are so many people and possibilities on offer. Allow for alterations to some of your schemes.

16 SATURDAY
Moon Age Day 5 • Moon Sign Gemini

am ....

pm ....

Unsettling events merely come along to prevent you getting yourself into a rut. Remember this fact today and you will be able to deal with all eventualities in a patient and reasonable manner. Life may not be quite as settled as you would wish, though it does have much to offer in a leisure and pleasure sense.

17 SUNDAY
Moon Age Day 6 • Moon Sign Cancer

am ....

pm ....

Make certain that you are on top of financial situations, right from the star. Of course you could always rely on the helpful suggestions of people in your vicinity, though they are not as likely as you are to make sensible decisions at present. Definitely a time to be backing your own hunches.

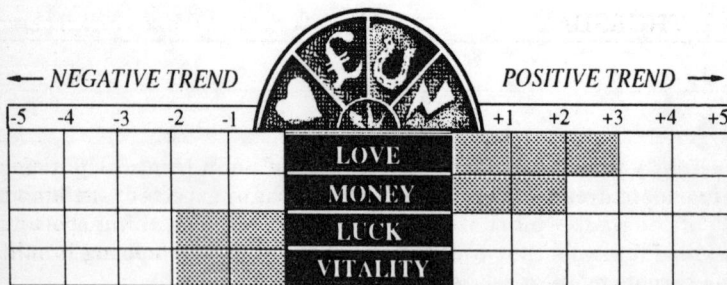

← *NEGATIVE TREND*　　　　　　　　*POSITIVE TREND* →

-5	-4	-3	-2	-1		+1	+2	+3	+4	+5
					LOVE					
					MONEY					
					LUCK					
					VITALITY					

18 MONDAY

Moon Age Day 7 • Moon Sign Cancer

am ....

pm ....

Domestic requirements can clash with social obligations at some stage today, and especially so since you are very busy trying to sort practical situations out too. Maybe you are just trying to do too much, and all at the same time. Just accept that you are only human and take all situations one at a time.

19 TUESDAY

Moon Age Day 8 • Moon Sign Cancer

am ....

pm ....

All social trends are well favoured, and it's a case of 'the more the merrier' when it comes to friendships. You want to feel that you are part of the group, though the reality of the situation is that you are right out there in front, doing much of the leading. New confidences can be expected.

20 WEDNESDAY

Moon Age Day 9 • Moon Sign Leo

am ....

pm ....

As the Sun enters your solar eighth house, so you are able to get shot of some worn-out concepts once and for all. Such situations are no longer very productive and during the next month or so the decks of your life are being cleared for a new form of activity, placing the emphasis more on your own choices.

21 THURSDAY

Moon Age Day 10 • Moon Sign Leo

am ....

pm ....

The influence of those around you really does begin to play a more important part in your life at present. Just be careful of the kind of criticism that you are willing to take on board however, because some of it really isn't fair. This is especially true, bearing in mind the direction it comes from.

22 FRIDAY

Moon Age Day 11 • Moon Sign Virgo

am ....

pm ....

Even the smallest details are of great importance when it comes to planning carefully for the future. This is where your patience comes in handy, because you are able to make the most of any opportunity right now and to pick the bones out of it. Stick to your own ideas whenever it proves to be possible.

23 SATURDAY

Moon Age Day 12 • Moon Sign Virgo

am ....

pm ....

The lunar high is with you again, this time bringing the very best time of the month for putting your plans into action and for persuading others that your ideas are the best ones around. Good luck is on your side and you are able to push it just a little harder than would usually be the case. Friends are very reasonable.

24 SUNDAY

Moon Age Day 13 • Moon Sign Libra

am ....

pm ....

You can take personal advantage of all possibilities today and will not be likely to lead yourself down any blind alleys. Confidence is quite high to do those things that you consider to be best suited to your variable and interesting nature. Popularity is certainly part of the gift on offer at present.

← *NEGATIVE TREND*   *POSITIVE TREND* →

-5	-4	-3	-2	-1		+1	+2	+3	+4	+5
					LOVE					
					MONEY					
					LUCK					
					VITALITY					

25 MONDAY
Moon Age Day 14 • Moon Sign Libra

am ....

pm ....

Unexpected financial gains could be on the way, but all the same, use your resources as wisely as you can today and don't go in for any over-ambitious schemes cooked up by people who really should know better. A potentially profitable period is on hand, though you could blow it by being impetuous.

26 TUESDAY
Moon Age Day 15 • Moon Sign Scorpio

am ....

pm ....

Communication with people out there in the big wide world are definitely to be favoured now. Perhaps there is a telephone call that you simply have to make, or someone who would be grateful to receive a letter from you. From a financial sense it would be wise to protect your interests for the moment.

27 WEDNESDAY
Moon Age Day 16 • Moon Sign Scorpio

am ....

pm ....

Mercury is now strong in your solar eighth house, which could indicate that your attentions are being turned towards personal problems and the way that you can more readily sort them out once and for all. Decision making is easy for most Librans this week, even if not everyone around you is inclined to agree.

28 THURSDAY
Moon Age Day 17 • Moon Sign Sagittarius

am ....

pm ....

Surprisingly, you discover today that your need for other people and for social contact generally is not half so high as you might have expected. Even so there are unique and stimulating events on offer, though you may have to go out and look for them much more than has been the case recently.

29 FRIDAY

Moon Age Day 18 • Moon Sign Sagittarius

am ....

pm ....

Those in your vicinity are quite clearly expecting more of you than you are willing or able to offer. Still, you can only be as forthcoming as your present nature will allow, a fact that the most important people in your life should easily be able to accept. Not a good day to allow others to make you feel guilty.

30 SATURDAY

Moon Age Day 19 • Moon Sign Capricorn

am ....

pm ....

A restful and relaxing day suits you down to the ground. While you are taking an hour or two to yourself, don't be surprised if loved ones have some unique ideas all of their own. A comfortable interlude is indicated, though one during which some of your thoughts will be turned in the direction of alterations.

1 SUNDAY

Moon Age Day 20 • Moon Sign Capricorn

am ....

pm ....

If you are the one at home who pulls the purse strings, this may not be a bad time to be getting out the treasure chest and for counting up the pennies. There are going to be one or two demands financially that you didn't expect, though this is no reason to avoid spoiling yourself just a little now.

← NEGATIVE TREND						POSITIVE TREND →				
-5	-4	-3	-2	-1		+1	+2	+3	+4	+5
					LOVE					
					MONEY					
					LUCK					
					VITALITY					

YOUR MONTH AT A GLANCE

The twelve numbered boxes represent the important areas in your life. The key to the numbers you will find beneath the panel. A Sun above the number indicates that opportunities are around. A Cloud below the number, that you should be a bit defensive. Nothing above or below and life will be pretty ordinary.

KEY

1 Strength of Personality
2 Personal Finance
3 Useful Information Gathering
4 Domestic Affairs
5 Pleasure & Romance
6 Effective Work & Health

7 One to One Relationships
8 Questioning, Thinking & Deciding
9 External Influences / Education
10 Career Aspirations
11 Teamwork Activities
12 Unconscious Impulses

MAY HIGHS AND LOWS

Here, I show how the rhythm of the Moon will affect you this month. Like the tide, your energies and abilities will rise and fall with its pattern. When it is above the date line, go-for-it. When it is below the line you should be resting.

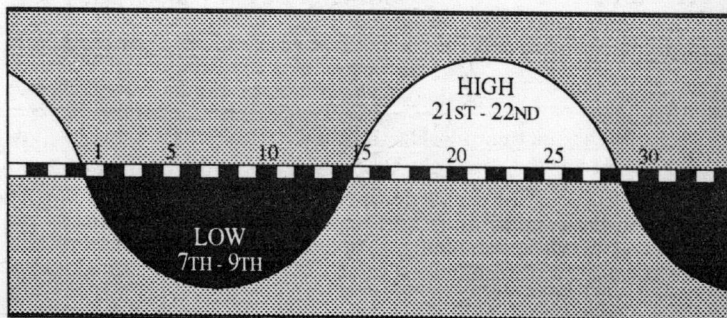

HIGH
21ST - 22ND

LOW
7TH - 9TH

2 MONDAY
Moon Age Day 21 • Moon Sign Aquarius

am ....

pm ....

The month of May suits you no end, after all no matter what the weather is doing at present, the best months of the year now lie ahead of you. Treat today as an exciting time to plan for the future, and as an interlude when you can help other people out, almost without trying to do so.

3 TUESDAY
Moon Age Day 22 • Moon Sign Aquarius

am ....

pm ....

Your usual routines are now left behind as you sail along on a tide of your own making. A change of scene would be very useful, though with a busy schedule surrounding you at present this could be more in your mind for the moment than in reality. News coming in from both near and far proves to be very interesting.

4 WEDNESDAY
Moon Age Day 23 • Moon Sign Aquarius

am ....

pm ....

The wheels of progress turn on, and now much more in your favour than may have been the case of late. Great things are on offer for those Librans who are willing to take a chance and deal with life in a sensible way. Not that you are being especially sensible when it comes to sorting out your personal life.

5 THURSDAY
Moon Age Day 24 • Moon Sign Pisces

am ....

pm ....

Issues from the past could arise and may force you into re-thinking certain aspects of the present. Be careful not to be too demanding of your partner, or others who take a great delight in being close to you. Not everyone you come across is equally useful or understanding, so extra effort is needed on your part.

6 FRIDAY
Moon Age Day 25 • Moon Sign Pisces

am ....

pm ....

It might seem that you are out of favour with certain people today, and if this is so, you can put the apparent fact down to the arrival of the lunar low. Don't take too much notice of it though because there are many situations about at present that look much better in another day or two.

7 SATURDAY
Moon Age Day 26 • Moon Sign Aries

am ....

pm ....

Personal and professional progress does not come to a halt, but is significantly slowed down now. All that you can really expect is that with patience, things will come good. In the meantime you may as well make the best of life and get some rest. Utilise your active imagination as much as you can.

8 SUNDAY
Moon Age Day 27 • Moon Sign Aries

am ....

pm ....

Emotional support is what you are looking for now, and in the main is what you should find. Those Librans who are involved in a permanent relationship should find that there is much help coming from the direction of their partner, though even those of you who are single can find a receptive ear.

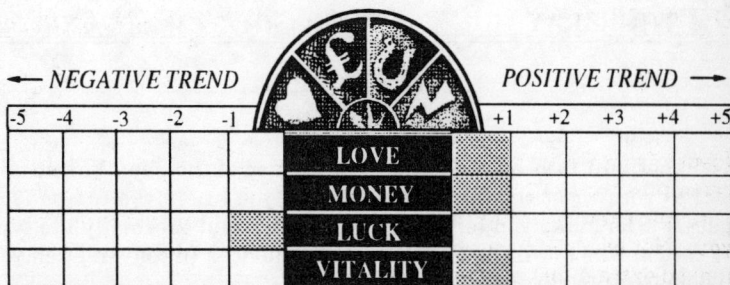

← NEGATIVE TREND   POSITIVE TREND →

-5	-4	-3	-2	-1			+1	+2	+3	+4	+5
					LOVE						
					MONEY						
					LUCK						
					VITALITY						

9 MONDAY

Moon Age Day 28 • Moon Sign Aries

am ....

pm ....

A meeting of minds now becomes much more likely, especially concerning matters of business. Even away from work it is amazing how much you can get on with people who have not seen your point of view in the past. Comfort and security could appear to be taking a back-seat for the next day or two.

10 TUESDAY

Moon Age Day 0 • Moon Sign Taurus

am ....

pm ....

Now you are taking a much more active role when it comes to sorting out the circumstances of your own life. Financially you should soon be in a much better position to please yourself. Personal attachments begin to make greater demands of you, though you can deal with these in a relaxed manner at present.

11 WEDNESDAY

Moon Age Day 1 • Moon Sign Taurus

am ....

pm ....

Not everyone you come across is in agreement with your ideas and principles just at present, so you will have to be at your usual tactful best. It should be possible with patience to bring most people round to your way of thinking, even though they could be radically opposed at the outset. Use circumstances to boost your own confidence.

12 THURSDAY

Moon Age Day 2 • Moon Sign Gemini

am ....

pm ....

The spotlight falls on the social possibilities of the day. You should feel at your most comfortable now when you are in the company of people who make you feel happy to be alive and especially the type of person who is willing to listen to your advice. In conversation you have plenty to say for yourself.

13 FRIDAY
Moon Age Day 3 • Moon Sign Gemini

am ....

pm ....

Who says that Friday the 13th has to be unlucky? This is not the case for you this time round at least, for with Venus in your solar ninth house you have a good day for getting things done, and for making the rounds of friends once the demands of the day have been left behind in a practical sense.

14 SATURDAY
Moon Age Day 4 • Moon Sign Gemini

am ....

pm ....

The present position of Mars in your chart could contribute to making you just a little more argumentative than would normally be the case. This is only likely to be a problem with regard to people who fail to appreciate that there is also a dynamic aspect to your nature. Try to explain yourself as fully as you can.

15 SUNDAY
Moon Age Day 5 • Moon Sign Cancer

am ....

pm ....

Although you can get a great deal from the social possibilities of this Spring Sunday, for many of you there is a tendency for your mind to turn towards matters practical and even professional. Loved-ones meanwhile could be a little over-anxious or even irritable. Get to the bottom of the problem and sort it out.

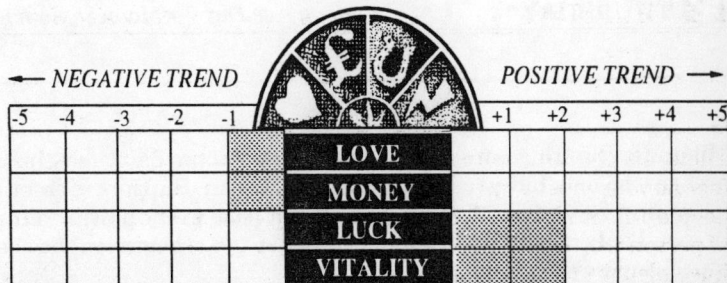

← NEGATIVE TREND							POSITIVE TREND →			
-5	-4	-3	-2	-1		+1	+2	+3	+4	+5
					LOVE					
					MONEY					
					LUCK					
					VITALITY					

16 MONDAY
Moon Age Day 6 • Moon Sign Cancer

am ....

pm ....

A fine day for sitting down and talking things through, no matter what the subject-matter may be. Your winning ways are much highlighted just now, so there is little reason for anyone to fall out with you at all. Where the disputes are not specifically yours, you should be able to see both points of view.

17 TUESDAY
Moon Age Day 7 • Moon Sign Leo

am ....

pm ....

With an opposition between the Sun and Pluto about , don't be surprised if many of your ideas fail to sound as reasonable just now as they may have done previously. Avoid confronting others with schemes that you know will not work to their favour as much as to your own.

18 WEDNESDAY
Moon Age Day 8 • Moon Sign Leo

am ....

pm ....

If there is any chance at all to get away from things now, you should grab the opportunity with both hands. You really are not in the mood for routines just now and would be in your element on a deserted beach or walking in the countryside. If a change is not possible, take at least a little time out.

19 THURSDAY
Moon Age Day 9 • Moon Sign Virgo

am ....

pm ....

Misunderstandings are all too likely in personal relationships at present, so do what you can to put them right. Support is on offer for radical new ideas of yours, though not from every possible direction and only of a limited sort. Keep one or two schemes on the shelf until you know the time is right.

20 FRIDAY

Moon Age Day 10 • Moon Sign Virgo

am ....

pm ....

A very charitable Libran greets the day, allowing you to feel that you can help almost anyone who seems to be a deserving case. Do make certain first that the people in question really do want the assistance that you are offering. The last thing that you would want right now would be to be accused of interfering.

21 SATURDAY

Moon Age Day 11 • Moon Sign Libra

am ....

pm ....

With the lunar high comes a physical peak and a feeling that you could move mountains. The advice is to take things steadily all the same because you won't get anywhere today by rushing your fences. Luck is on your side and you can be bold in your determination to make others listen to your plans.

22 SUNDAY

Moon Age Day 12 • Moon Sign Libra

am ....

pm ....

Everyday matters should be running quite smoothly, allowing more time for you to concentrate on specific issues that are close to your heart. If you feel like a little flutter of some sort, this could be the time, but remember that yours is not the luckiest of signs financially, so some care is still necessary.

← *NEGATIVE TREND*   *POSITIVE TREND* →

-5	-4	-3	-2	-1		+1	+2	+3	+4	+5
					LOVE					
					MONEY					
					LUCK					
					VITALITY					

23 MONDAY
Moon Age Day 13 • Moon Sign Scorpio

am ....

pm ....

The Sun takes a trip into your solar ninth house, expanding your horizons no end. Others want to be part of what they see to be a winning nature, and though you are always generous, it might not be such a good idea to allow them all the credit for things that you manage to sort out on your own.

24 TUESDAY
Moon Age Day 14 • Moon Sign Scorpio

am ....

pm ....

The simple pleasures of life are certainly the ones that appeal to you the most now. The last thing that you would be looking for would be complications of any sort, even if one or two seem to find you of their own accord. Remain as open as you can to any new experience that comes your way.

25 WEDNESDAY
Moon Age Day 15 • Moon Sign Sagittarius

am ....

pm ....

News that you have been expecting may not turn out to be quite as hopeful as you may have wished. A few set-backs should not stop the forward progress that you are enjoying, however, and it could be that you stop at barricades which are only in your own mind. The more positive you manage to be, the better. —

26 THURSDAY
Moon Age Day 16 • Moon Sign Sagittarius

am ....

pm ....

Self-determination can now see you managing to sort out problems that have been on the periphery of your life for quite some time. Avoid being more hard-headed than you would normally be when dealing with others because this can only lead to problems further down the line. Loved ones especially need the kind of support you offer.

27 FRIDAY
Moon Age Day 17 • Moon Sign Capricorn

am ....

pm ....

At the end of the working week you can focus your mind totally on career prospects and what you can do to make them more appealing. Once work is out of the way, however, you should do your best to make some space for yourself socially. The one thing that is certainly not lacking at present is popularity.

28 SATURDAY
Moon Age Day 18 • Moon Sign Capricorn

am ....

pm ....

If there are minor problems at home it would be a good idea to nip them in the bud as early in the day as you are able. Family issues are a little tense, but since this is mainly thanks to the attitudes and behaviour of others, there is nothing that you really have to take yourself to task about.

29 SUNDAY
Moon Age Day 19 • Moon Sign Capricorn

am ....

pm ....

Communicate with as many people as you can. Some really good incentives come out of even apparently idle gossip and almost everyone you meet is anxious to help you out in one way or another. You should now be able to see much more clearly the direction that your mind is taking, even if you cannot really influence things.

← *NEGATIVE TREND*   *POSITIVE TREND* →

-5	-4	-3	-2	-1			+1	+2	+3	+4	+5
				▓	LOVE						
					MONEY	▓					
			▓		LUCK						
		▓	▓		VITALITY						

30 MONDAY
Moon Age Day 20 • Moon Sign Aquqrius

am ....

pm ....

Social gatherings are apt to create potential flash-point situations, which you will have to deal with. Keeping warring parties away from each other is part of what your sign has been doing since the dawn of time. You are a natural diplomat and can easily sort things out, without becoming personally involved.

31 TUESDAY
Moon Age Day 21 • Moon Sign Aquqrius

am ....

pm ....

What a busy Libran you are today. In fact there is so much to do that you scarcely have the chance to stop and take breath. If this is the case, perhaps you should take the time to ask yourself if one or two things might not be best left until a later date. At least that way you could concentrate more.

1 WEDNESDAY
Moon Age Day 22 • Moon Sign Pisces

am ....

pm ....

Most financial situations are positively highlighted, though you do have a powerful opposition of Mars and Jupiter in your chart today and this can mean that at least some money matters do need an especially careful form of handling. Opportunities for new and unexpected gains cannot be ruled out now.

2 THURSDAY
Moon Age Day 23 • Moon Sign Pisces

am ....

pm ....

Tried and tested paths are the really important ones to be taking now. You should be able to branch out into new areas of life and to force your mind down paths that you would usually avoid. Disagreements at home in the days ahead can be dealt with in no time at all, even if certain other parties are inclined to work against you.

3 FRIDAY
Moon Age Day 24 • Moon Sign Aries

am ....

pm ....

It may appear that you are getting a slightly raw deal from some aspects of life. If this turns out to be the case, then you would be well advised to think again. It is not always the direct approach to situations that works to your advantage just now, so try to be a little more devious than you would usually be.

4 SATURDAY
Moon Age Day 25 • Moon Sign Aries

am ....

pm ....

Your thinking is greatly affected by personal situations, and it might be an idea to put them to the back of your mind, at least when you are dealing with practical situations. Don't make life easy for others if to do so means that your own way of going on is shot to pieces. Attitude is all-important in friendships.

5 SUNDAY
Moon Age Day 26 • Moon Sign Aries

am ....

pm...

A positive spotlight is turned onto all travel matters and arrangements for family outings, no matter if they are being undertaken now or in the future. All social encounters should be quite fulfilling, which is why you are so keen to mix and mingle with as many people as you can. Arguments are for others today, not for you.

← *NEGATIVE TREND*   *POSITIVE TREND* →

-5	-4	-3	-2	-1		+1	+2	+3	+4	+5
					LOVE					
					MONEY					
					LUCK					
					VITALITY					

JUNE

1994

YOUR MONTH AT A GLANCE

The twelve numbered boxes represent the important areas in your life.
The key to the numbers you will find beneath the panel. A Sun above
the number indicates that opportunities are around. A Cloud below
the number, that you should be a bit defensive. Nothing above or
below and life will be pretty ordinary.

KEY

1 Strength of Personality	7 One to One Relationships
2 Personal Finance	8 Questioning, Thinking & Deciding
3 Useful Information Gathering	9 External Influences / Education
4 Domestic Affairs	10 Career Aspirations
5 Pleasure & Romance	11 Teamwork Activities
6 Effective Work & Health	12 Unconscious Impulses

JUNE HIGHS AND LOWS

Here, I show how the rhythm of the Moon will affect you this month.
Like the tide, your energies and abilities will rise and fall with its pattern. When it is above the date line, go-for-it. When it is below the
line you should be resting.

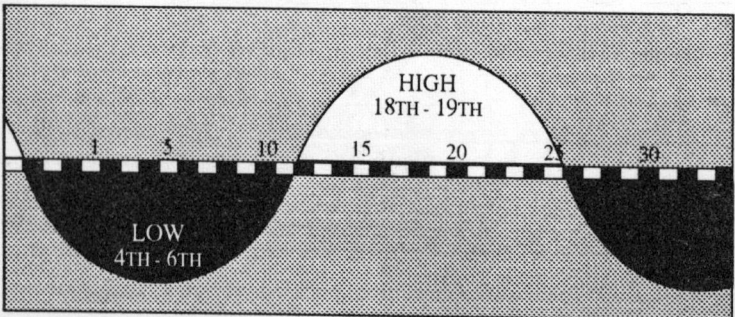

HIGH
18TH - 19TH

LOW
4TH - 6TH

6 MONDAY
Moon Age Day 27 • Moon Sign Taurus

am ....

pm ....

Some important career moves may not be all that far away now and it would be worth looking at the options carefully before you allow yourself to make any irrevocable decision. In terms of popularity you should now be reaching a peak and can even have a good talk to people who do not usually understand you.

7 TUESDAY
Moon Age Day 28 • Moon Sign Taurus

am ....

pm ....

A day of fairly unusual happenings and possibly one or two dramatic encounters too. This would not be a good interlude for taking chances financially, so look after your hard-earned cash as much as you can for the moment. Look carefully at relationships that may have been going wrong recently.

8 WEDNESDAY
Moon Age Day 29 • Moon Sign Gemini

am ....

pm ....

Although you have a tendency to speak first and think about the consequences later just at the moment, you also have enough cheek and sufficient diplomacy to get you out of any potential difficulty as a result. You are looking for new and exciting possibilities in your life, even if friends have other plans.

9 THURSDAY
Moon Age Day 0 • Moon Sign Gemini

am ....

pm ....

You cannot prepare for every eventuality that life may throw in your path, though you are looking ahead very well at present and should be able to arrange things better than even you expect. Together with your friends you are able to put new incentives into operation, which could mean a little excitement.

10 FRIDAY
Moon Age Day 1 • Moon Sign Gemini

am ....

pm ....

Socially speaking there are likely to be some people who you just can't manage to get along with, no matter how much you try to do so. Intimate relationships are a different matter altogether however and respond well to your romantic and very positive approach. A good day for receiving and giving compliments.

11 SATURDAY
Moon Age Day 2 • Moon Sign Cancer

am ....

pm..

It is very rare that your natural attitude would give offence to other people, after all you are known as the best diplomat in the zodiac. Despite this, even you can have days when it would be best to keep quiet rather than to give offence. In some ways, this is such a period, though more in casual rather than personal situations.

12 SUNDAY
Moon Age Day 3 • Moon Sign Cancer

am ....

pm..

You can have a real calming influence on the people you live with now, in direct contradiction to some of the possible happenings of yesterday. The reason in a positive aspect in your chart between the planets Mercury and Pluto. Money matters show considerable improvement, even if you have to wait a while for it.

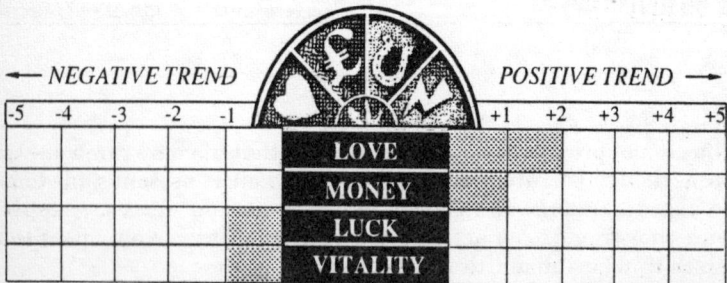

← *NEGATIVE TREND*   *POSITIVE TREND* →

-5	-4	-3	-2	-1			+1	+2	+3	+4	+5
					LOVE						
					MONEY						
					LUCK						
					VITALITY						

13 MONDAY
Moon Age Day 4 • Moon Sign Leo

am ....

pm ....

No sooner do you get yourself out into the mainstream of another busy week than you find that much of your attention is being turned back towards the needs and wants that people at home have of you. Finding the right sort of balance may not be especially easy today, but it is very necessary.

14 TUESDAY
Moon Age Day 5 • Moon Sign Leo

am ....

pm ....

You should be able to strike a happy medium now between catering for the needs that your nearest and dearest have of you and also fulfilling your expectations of yourself professionally. A friend may be invaluable when it comes to offering you just the right advice at the correct moment.

15 WEDNESDAY
Moon Age Day 6 • Moon Sign Virgo

am ....

pm ....

Sweet Venus enters your solar eleventh house today, improving your openness and your friendly approach to just about everyone you come across. Personal plans and aspirations need looking at rather closely, especially since you now have much more enterprise and openness than has been the case for a while.

16 THURSDAY
Moon Age Day 7 • Moon Sign Virgo

am ....

pm ....

Resist the urge to dwell on the past, because although certain aspects of it do seem to find you out on a number of occasions today, to worry about it really would not be much use. In some respects you will be doing all that you can to maintain a low profile at present, which could come as a surprise to others.

17 FRIDAY

Moon Age Day 8 • Moon Sign Virgo

am ....

pm ....

The lunar high is of use to you now and you find that you are embarking on a significant winning streak in many spheres of your life. Probably the only potential problem is taking on more than you know to be good for you. This could be especially evident at work, where you may try to sort everything prior to the weekend.

18 SATURDAY

Moon Age Day 9 • Moon Sign Libra

am ....

pm ....

Professional matters now take a back-seat, as many Librans settle into what should be an interesting and positive sort of weekend. No matter how many other issues may cross your mind at present, the most important factor is your social life. Now is a time to shine out in company and to make heads turn.

19 SUNDAY

Moon Age Day 10 • Moon Sign Libra

am ....

pm ....

In a financial sense, you now show a tendency to go to extremes, something that you would probably avoid if you took the trouble to think things through correctly. There is some useful advice about in a more personal sense, though you might find it hard to listen to contrary opinions at present.

← *NEGATIVE TREND*   *POSITIVE TREND* →

-5	-4	-3	-2	-1			+1	+2	+3	+4	+5
					LOVE						
					MONEY						
					LUCK						
					VITALITY						

20 MONDAY   *Moon Age Day 11 • Moon Sign Scorpio*

am ....

pm ....

Where important personal decisions are concerned, it would be a good idea to defer some of them until a little later, even though with the Moon now in your solar second house, these are the issues that crop up time and again. In a financial sense there may be a need for some cutbacks, even if these are only temporary.

21 TUESDAY   *Moon Age Day 12 • Moon Sign Scorpio*

am ....

pm ....

You occupy an important position as far as family matters are concerned, so that others are taking more notice of you than you would normally give yourself credit for. The truth is that you play more of a part in the decision making of people generally than you are willing to believe, which is quite a responsibility.

22 WEDNESDAY   *Moon Age Day 13 • Moon Sign Sagittarius*

am ....

pm ....

Most meetings, appointments and travel arrangements go according to plan and this should not be a day when life is throwing any sort of obstacle in your path. Any journey that you do make today probably won't be especially long in terms of duration, though you do not have to go far now to enjoy yourself.

23 THURSDAY   *Moon Age Day 14 • Moon Sign Sagittarius*

am ....

pm ....

There is a positive focus on money-matters and a need to sort out today's complications before you move on to any for the future. The people in your immediate vicinity seem more than willing to settle for what you believe, even if they have different ideas themselves. Officials could be very demanding.

24 FRIDAY
Moon Age Day 15 • Moon Sign Capricorn

am ....

pm ....

There is a busy atmosphere around, so much so that it is very unlikely that you would get through everything that is of importance to you just at present. Priorities need to be sorted out as quickly as possible because you do need some sort of routine to work towards. Personal frustrations can be resolved.

25 SATURDAY
Moon Age Day 16 • Moon Sign Capricorn

am ....

pm ....

The needs of the day from a practical point of view look like interfering with what should also be an important social interlude. It would be sensible to look at all situations carefully before proceeding. You may be taking on a number of responsibilities that have little to do with you personally.

26 SUNDAY
Moon Age Day 17 • Moon Sign Aquarius

am ....

pm ....

Now more interested than ever to know what makes other people tick, do what you can to help out but avoid becoming involved in the complicated lives of people who you will never really be able to understand. High spirits are in evidence and leisure interests could predominate, especially later in the day.

← NEGATIVE TREND							*POSITIVE TREND →*			
-5	-4	-3	-2	-1		+1	+2	+3	+4	+5
					LOVE					
					MONEY					
					LUCK					
					VITALITY					

27 MONDAY
Moon Age Day 18 • Moon Sign Aquarius

am ....

pm ....

A combination of Mars and the planet Uranus make you decide that your ideas are not so strange after all. In fact almost anything is worth a second look now, in contrast to last week when you were more inclined to find value in ideas from outside. Convincing others that you are correct is where your energies should be placed.

28 TUESDAY
Moon Age Day 19 • Moon Sign Pisces

am ....

pm ....

Attracting the help of friends and acquaintances is easy, even if outsiders are not so simple to come to terms with. This would not be an ideal period for deciding to go it alone work-wise, and co-operation works wonders. A very talkative Libran greets the day, making all communication with others easy.

29 WEDNESDAY
Moon Age Day 20 • Moon Sign Pisces

am ....

pm ....

In situations where you know that others are more knowledgeable than you are it would be a good idea to defer to their choices. This is a period when too many cooks definitely could spoil the broth, not a situation that would prove to be very helpful in the fullness of time. Patience is hard to find.

30 THURSDAY
Moon Age Day 21 • Moon Sign Pisces

am ....

pm ....

It would be best to maintain a rather low profile just for the moment. The lunar low should not be too difficult to deal with this time round, though it could still stop you in your tracks concerning projects and ideas that are close to your heart. Negative moods become slightly more likely than usual.

1 FRIDAY

Moon Age Day 22 • Moon Sign Aries

am ....

pm ....

It's hard to make everything work out exactly the way that you would wish it to do right now, and the secret probably is not to try. Life jogs along well enough as long as you resist the urge to interfere with it, something that all air sign people find difficult. Friends have good reasons for their behaviour.

2 SATURDAY

Moon Age Day 23 • Moon Sign Aries

am ....

pm ....

Not a good period for building up your hopes in practical matters, though an excellent time for planning rather than doing. Contradictions in the behaviour of those around you could have more to do with the way that you are looking at life than they do with reality. Try to take an impartial point of view if you can.

3 SUNDAY

Moon Age Day 24 • Moon Sign Taurus

am ....

pm ....

Mars enters your solar ninth house, stimulating a number of important debates and gradually making you more dynamic in your approach to life than would often be the case. Now you become much more competitive in your associations with others, not something that they understand unless you are able to explain yourself.

← *NEGATIVE TREND*   *POSITIVE TREND* →

-5	-4	-3	-2	-1		+1	+2	+3	+4	+5
					LOVE					
					MONEY					
					LUCK					
					VITALITY					

JULY

1994

YOUR MONTH AT A GLANCE

The twelve numbered boxes represent the important areas in your life. The key to the numbers you will find beneath the panel. A Sun above the number indicates that opportunities are around. A Cloud below the number, that you should be a bit defensive. Nothing above or below and life will be pretty ordinary.

1	2	3	4	5	6	7	8	9	10	11	12

KEY

1 Strength of Personality
2 Personal Finance
3 Useful Information Gathering
4 Domestic Affairs
5 Pleasure & Romance
6 Effective Work & Health

7 One to One Relationships
8 Questioning, Thinking & Deciding
9 External Influences / Education
10 Career Aspirations
11 Teamwork Activities
12 Unconscious Impulses

JULY HIGHS AND LOWS

Here, I show how the rhythm of the Moon will affect you this month. Like the tide, your energies and abilities will rise and fall with its pattern. When it is above the date line, go-for-it. When it is below the line you should be resting.

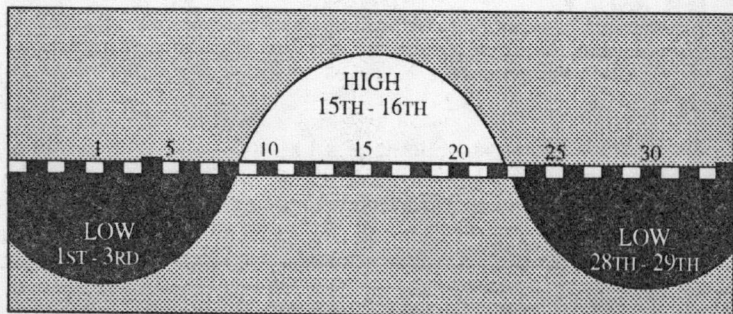

HIGH
15TH - 16TH

LOW
1ST - 3RD

LOW
28TH - 29TH

4 MONDAY
Moon Age Day 25 • Moon Sign Taurus

am ....

pm...

Although many of your plans for the future, regarding work and all practical issues, may be in generally good order, they may still need some careful thought today. Some further preparations could be necessary regarding intended changes to routines at work. Social prospects tend to improve.

5 TUESDAY
Moon Age Day 26 • Moon Sign Taurus

am ....

pm...

Despite the natural enthusiasm that attends your life today, don't be at all surprised if certain other people seem determined to take a point of view that is contrary to your own. Bring a little change into your life as far as out-of-work activities are concerned, you don't want to be accused of being tedious.

6 WEDNESDAY
Moon Age Day 27 • Moon Sign Gemini

am ....

pm ....

The usual Libran easy-going charm is more in evidence than ever today, thanks to the present position of your ruler, Venus, in your solar eleventh house. If invitations come in for a closer involvement in group activities of one sort or another, look at them carefully before dismissing them out of hand.

7 THURSDAY
Moon Age Day 28 • Moon Sign Gemini

am ....

pm ....

Your career and long-term plans of all kinds can now be helped by people who put themselves in a position of influence with regard to your life. Even the most unlikely types now stand behind you and should be willing to be counted if there are any small upheavals. You present an attractive figure to most people now.

8 FRIDAY

Moon Age Day 0 • Moon Sign Cancer

am ....

pm ....

Minor though positive results come about regarding the real effort you have put in recently to get ahead in your life as a whole. Of course, nothing is going to happen quite as quickly as you would wish just at the moment, because your usual patience appears to be taking a holiday. You could do with a break yourself!

9 SATURDAY

Moon Age Day 1 • Moon Sign Cancer

am ....

pm ....

An excellent day for travel and for broadening your horizons, definitely not a time for sitting around and waiting for something exciting to happen. There are certainly no lack of possibilities around just at present, though you will have to go out and grab them by the scruff of the neck.

10 SUNDAY

Moon Age Day 2 • Moon Sign Leo

am ....

pm ....

A testing time comes along from a practical point of view, thanks to an association of Mars and Jupiter. It really is a case of getting on with those things that you know you can deal with easily, and not a time for allowing yourself to be held back by negative statements or attitudes from the direction of others.

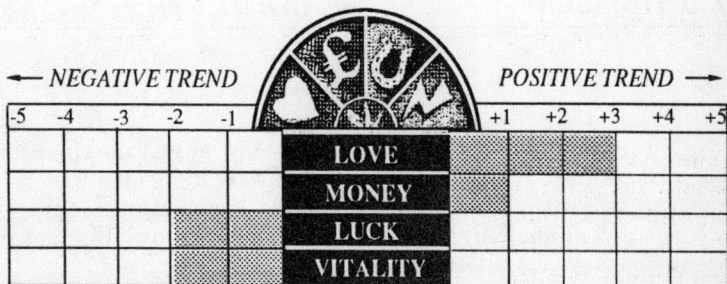

← *NEGATIVE TREND*   *POSITIVE TREND* →

-5	-4	-3	-2	-1		+1	+2	+3	+4	+5
					LOVE					
					MONEY					
					LUCK					
					VITALITY					

11 MONDAY
Moon Age Day 3 • Moon Sign Leo

am ....

pm..

Determination becomes a temporary and quite welcome weapon in your arsenal. Of course this will not go down especially well with everyone, after all you are usually so willing to go with the flow. It isn't always a bad thing to surprise people however, and you may jog friends into some positive actions.

12 TUESDAY
Moon Age Day 4 • Moon Sign Leo

am ....

pm..

You may desire seclusion and privacy from an outside world that is looking just a tiny bit threatening from your side of the fence. Perhaps you have walked a little further out onto the stage of life than you normally would, and as a result could feel somewhat vulnerable. Smile at the impulsiveness of friends.

13 WEDNESDAY
Moon Age Day 5 • Moon Sign Virgo

am ....

pm ....

With Venus now starting to occupy your solar twelfth house, you should find that certain relationships are apt to place a strain on you that you could well do without. However, there is no planetary position that is inherently bad, and this one also brings more determination to come to terms with awkward types.

14 THURSDAY
Moon Age Day 6 • Moon Sign Virgo

am ....

pm ....

You return to a high-spirited approach today, at just the right time because you are being watched very closely by people who have some significant influence in your future. People want to invest in you one way or another, and could be offering responsibility that you want, but may be a little afraid of.

15 FRIDAY
Moon Age Day 7 • Moon Sign Libra

am ....

pm ....

The lunar high always spells success of one sort or another, though this time around it might also mean that you have to be a little more careful in your approach to others. The problem is that what you say, and what you mean, could come out sounding like two very different things. Diplomacy is called for.

16 SATURDAY
Moon Age Day 8 • Moon Sign Libra

am ....

pm ....

An association of Venus and Jupiter makes it possible, and advantageous, to concentrate on matters close to your heart. Money matters improve, perhaps partly thanks to the help and support that comes from the directions of others. Figures from the past could show again in your life and be utilised in assessing the future.

17 SUNDAY
Moon Age Day 9 • Moon Sign Scorpio

am ....

pm ....

Events at home could be rather unsettling, though the aspect that is creating this situation is neither very powerful or particularly long in duration. For your own part, you can be rather more irritable than would generally be the case, and will need to exercise a little caution, even in casual conversations.

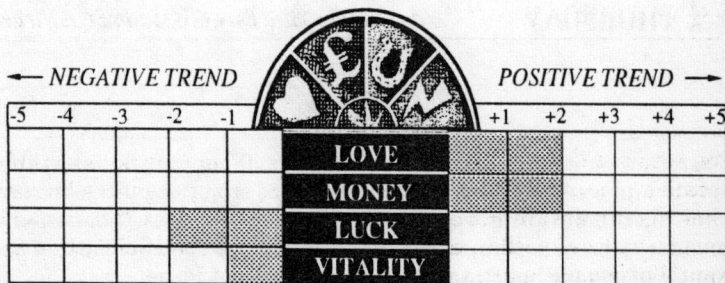

← NEGATIVE TREND						POSITIVE TREND →				
-5	-4	-3	-2	-1		+1	+2	+3	+4	+5
					LOVE					
					MONEY					
					LUCK					
					VITALITY					

18 MONDAY   *Moon Age Day 10 • Moon Sign Scorpio*

am ....

pm..

Hitches to plans are soon dealt with, and in any case the main emphasis today is placed upon indulging yourself in one way or another. There ought to be the chance to get some time to be alone with your thoughts and to meditate on things from the past. It is important not to dwell on them too much, though.

19 TUESDAY   *Moon Age Day 11 • Moon Sign Sagittarius*

am ....

pm..

A busy and eventful day, when you are doing all that you can to be of assistance to others. Take things steadily all the same because there will be no prizes awarded for rushing about at present. Others can seem to be rather distant and need the special approach that is almost second nature to you. Friends seek you out.

20 WEDNESDAY   *Moon Age Day 12 • Moon Sign Sagittarius*

am ....

pm ....

Mars and Saturn combine to throw a spanner in the works when it comes to making things work out in the way that you would wish. Put aspects of past efforts behind you, especially concerning those occasions when things did not turn out as you would have wished. What matters is your effort now and in the future.

21 THURSDAY   *Moon Age Day 13 • Moon Sign Capricorn*

am ....

pm ....

There are some obstacles about at present, though if you take things slowly and steadily there should be little to stop the general momentum that is building up in your life. Don't expect those in your vicinity to be as enthusiastic as you are about specific matters that are close to your heart, they may have different ideas.

22 FRIDAY
Moon Age Day 14 • Moon Sign Capricorn

am ....

pm ....

Cheerful events at home turn your gaze in that direction, and you probably find yourself becoming more involved in certain ventures than you originally intended. More time and energy needs to be put into romantic possibilities as you approach a period of hearts and flowers. Make your personal feelings well known.

23 SATURDAY
Moon Age Day 15 • Moon Sign Aquarius

am ....

pm ....

The Sun moves on into your solar eleventh house, bringing a period of significant reward over the next month or so, and especially regarding friendships. A more charitable Libran begins to emerge, making it easy for you to help others out, and possibly to become involved in a more structured form of giving.

24 SUNDAY
Moon Age Day 16 • Moon Sign Aquarius

am ....

pm ....

Serious issues have to be dealt with from a personal point-of-view, though this does not mean that you must be sombre in your attitude. The power of your personality is evident to most people and you may choose to mix with one or two individuals today who do not usually play such an important part in your life.

◄— *NEGATIVE TREND*   *POSITIVE TREND* —►

-5	-4	-3	-2	-1		+1	+2	+3	+4	+5
					LOVE					
					MONEY					
					LUCK					
					VITALITY					

25 MONDAY
Moon Age Day 17 • Moon Sign Aquarius

am ....

pm...

The remarks of others, which are not designed to make you feel exactly on top of the world, are probably made without any real thought as to your reaction. By all means make it plain that you are not exactly over the moon, but avoid today's predisposition towards sulking, which is not really your style at all.

26 TUESDAY
Moon Age Day 18 • Moon Sign Pisces

am ....

pm...

A contact between Mercury and Mars indicates that you have plenty to say for yourself, but also shows that not everyone you meet is going to fall in line with what you believe immediately. It might be a good idea to work hard at getting your message across all the same. New social circles could be beckoning later.

27 WEDNESDAY
Moon Age Day 19 • Moon Sign Pisces

am ....

pm ....

The lunar low arrives, though such is the momentum of your life at present that you are unable to stop events rolling forward in any case. You may choose to be an observer on the bus of life just now, since you are less inclined to feel that you are up at the front driving. There should be plenty to take your fancy.

28 THURSDAY
Moon Age Day 20 • Moon Sign Aries

am ....

pm ....

Not a time to be forcing issues, as once again you are content to let things unfold as they should. The desire to interfere is part of what you are as an air sign, but this does not have to be a seven-day-a-week situation. The more rest you are able to get now, the greater will be your enjoyment of the weekend.

29 FRIDAY

Moon Age Day 21 • Moon Sign Aries

am ....

pm ....

You are at a disadvantage regarding personal interests at the start of today, since you may feel that others are not really pulling their weight in the way that you would wish. However, your enthusiasm for life is certain to win out in the end and you can easily persuade others that your point-of-view is sound.

30 SATURDAY

Moon Age Day 22 • Moon Sign Taurus

am ....

pm ....

Mercury, together with the planet Uranus, makes your home environment a hive of activity. You may choose to stand back and watch in amazement as people go flying about, and perhaps you are not really in the mood to join in as much as you normally would. Social confusion commencing today could take a while to clear up.

31 SUNDAY

Moon Age Day 23 • Moon Sign Taurus

am ....

pm ....

A busy day, and one that could tie you to routine matters unless you take a conscious decision to do only what takes your fancy. Having spent a large part of the week helping others out and doing those things you thought to be necessary for the general good, now you have more time to think about yourself.

← NEGATIVE TREND						POSITIVE TREND →				
-5	-4	-3	-2	-1		+1	+2	+3	+4	+5
					LOVE					
					MONEY					
					LUCK					
					VITALITY					

1994

YOUR MONTH AT A GLANCE

The twelve numbered boxes represent the important areas in your life.
The key to the numbers you will find beneath the panel. A Sun above
the number indicates that opportunities are around. A Cloud below
the number, that you should be a bit defensive. Nothing above or
below and life will be pretty ordinary.

1	2	3	4	5	6	7	8	9	10	11	12

KEY

1 Strength of Personality
2 Personal Finance
3 Useful Information Gathering
4 Domestic Affairs
5 Pleasure & Romance
6 Effective Work & Health

7 One to One Relationships
8 Questioning, Thinking & Deciding
9 External Influences / Education
10 Career Aspirations
11 Teamwork Activities
12 Unconscious Impulses

AUGUST HIGHS AND LOWS

Here, I show how the rhythm of the Moon will affect you this month.
Like the tide, your energies and abilities will rise and fall with its pattern. When it is above the date line, go-for-it. When it is below the
line you should be resting.

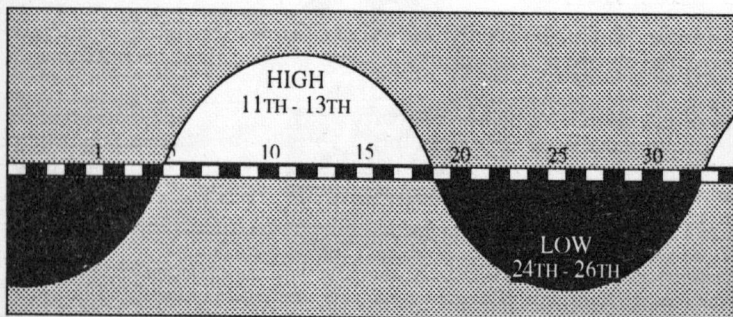

HIGH
11TH - 13TH

1   10   15   20   25   30

LOW
24TH - 26TH

1 MONDAY
Moon Age Day 24 • Moon Sign Taurus

am ....

pm ....

Mars in your solar ninth house at the beginning of August is almost certain to bring a desire for fresh fields and pastures new. You should be on the lookout for new faces to stimulate you generally and could also be hankering after travel, especially if circumstances have tied you to the same spot recently.

2 TUESDAY
Moon Age Day 25 • Moon Sign Gemini

am ....

pm ....

Keeping abreast of short-term career developments can be a real trial just now, and you may decide to abandon the quest for at least a while. There are certain advantages to be gained from going with the flow for now, not least of all taking time to look at your personal and social life in a little more detail.

3 WEDNESDAY
Moon Age Day 26 • Moon Sign Gemini

am ....

pm ....

Mercury now enters your solar eleventh house, bringing a new period of bright and breezy happenings and better powers of communication. With a definite preference for casual acquaintances, instead of some of the intensity that has occupied many Librans recently, you should be happy to laze around a little too.

4 THURSDAY
Moon Age Day 27 • Moon Sign Cancer

am ....

pm ....

There is an essential dilemma in your mind at present. Do you carry on with a thousand-and-one domestic duties that you know to be of supreme importance at present, or should you decide to leave things alone for a day or two and have a well-earned rest? Well, of course the choice has to be yours, but some things could wait for a while!

137

5 FRIDAY
Moon Age Day 28 • Moon Sign Cancer

am ....

pm ....

Life now appears to be a bit less stop-start and should offer you more chance to relate on aspects or happening with others in the mainstream of events. Libran friendliness is never far from the surface and this does allow for more in the way of genuine popularity than you may feel to have been the case.

6 SATURDAY
Moon Age Day 29 • Moon Sign Cancer

am ....

pm ....

Deeper and more emotional issues now rise to the surface, causing you to look carefully at relationships and to work out ways to make life more secure. In fact things are probably quite good at the moment and it is only your point of perspective that is a little wrong. Certainly a time to relax.

7 SUNDAY
Moon Age Day 0 • Moon Sign Leo

am ....

pm ....

Venus leaves your solar twelfth house behind and moves into your first house today. This is an important happening because it removes some of the restrictions that seem to have caused one or two problems in your personal life of late and should allow you to express your emotions more fully in the weeks ahead.

← *NEGATIVE TREND*   *POSITIVE TREND* →

-5	-4	-3	-2	-1			+1	+2	+3	+4	+5
					LOVE						
					MONEY						
					LUCK						
					VITALITY						

8 MONDAY
Moon Age Day 1 • Moon Sign Leo

am ....

pm ....

Challenges are almost inevitable at the start on a new and more exciting working week. Most of these you will rise to with very little difficulty at all, but don't expect to get on well with everyone you come across. Some people are just alien to your sort of nature, no matter how kind and giving you try to be.

9 TUESDAY
Moon Age Day 2 • Moon Sign Virgo

am ....

pm ....

A slightly cooler approach to the people you deal with every day can now be put down to the position of Mercury in your eleventh house. Where disputes or arguments have occurred in the recent past, it should become possible to put things right, though you tend to do so with a more clinical sort of behaviour.

10 WEDNESDAY
Moon Age Day 3 • Moon Sign Virgo

am ....

pm ....

Look out for trips down memory lane. These may not appear at first sight to be of very much use to you, though you might be slightly wrong. The truth is that what worked well for you in the past could well do so again now. Your attachment to specific people could come as a surprise to others in your life.

11 THURSDAY
Moon Age Day 4 • Moon Sign Libra

am ....

pm ....

Along with the lunar high comes more enthusiasm and the ability to put yourself to the front in new endeavours. Enthusiasm is more in evidence than would have been the case previously and there are a wealth of people who should now be more than willing to follow your lead. Plan early for the weekend ahead.

12 FRIDAY
Moon Age Day 5 • Moon Sign Libra

am ....

pm ....

The things you have to say to those people who mean the most to you today will certainly not fall on deaf ears, in fact you could be very surprised with the reactions that are coming your way. Sympathy abounds for the underdog and this is an interlude when you will be doing all that you can for others generally.

13 SATURDAY
Moon Age Day 6 • Moon Sign Scorpio

am ....

pm ....

Friends and relatives alike now seem to doing all that they can to interfere in your life. The real problem here lies in knowing who genuinely wants to be of help to you and who is merely trying to stick their nose in where it is not needed or wanted. Past issues can be confronted with confidence.

14 SUNDAY
Moon Age Day 7 • Moon Sign Scorpio

am ....

pm ....

Now determined to make practical progress whenever you can, you will not want to spend too much time dreaming. Since your nearest and dearest appear to have very different ideas it would seem to be a good idea to search for a compromise of some sort. Beware of being self-indulgent later.

← *NEGATIVE TREND*   *POSITIVE TREND* →

-5	-4	-3	-2	-1		+1	+2	+3	+4	+5
					LOVE					
					MONEY					
					LUCK					
					VITALITY					

15 MONDAY
Moon Age Day 8 • Moon Sign Sagittarius

am ....

pm ....

News that you receive today could turn out to be something of a disappointment, that is until you choose to look at it more carefully than has been the case in the past. A fresh course of action now needs to be considered and you will have to plan again. Such a situation does lead to more radical views.

16 TUESDAY
Moon Age Day 9 • Moon Sign Sagittarius

am ....

pm ....

Fiery Mars takes a journey into your solar tenth house today, bringing a new period for being in the driving-seat. Professional ambitions become much more important and although you are still willing to find some sort of compromise on most occasions, it's true that you can become just a little more selfish.

17 WEDNESDAY
Moon Age Day 10 • Moon Sign Sagittarius

am ....

pm ....

Rewarding encounters help you to make the most out of your love life, and could cheer up the middle of the week no end. Romance proves to be an important factor in the day, even for those Librans who may consider themselves to be more than settled at present. Casual conversations turn out to be very important.

18 THURSDAY
Moon Age Day 11 • Moon Sign Capricorn

am ....

pm ....

With the emphasis on private matters from the past, you should do everything that you can to ensure continuity in your present life and no preoccupation with events that have gone for ever. There is no point in dwelling on things at present and a genuine commitment to what lies ahead would be the best solution.

19 FRIDAY

Moon Age Day 12 • Moon Sign Capricorn

am ....

pm ....

Romantic and love issues certainly do bring out the best in you. High spirits are shared by everyone in your vicinity and there could be special interest coming from people who have done their best to support you in the past. These same people look like becoming more important in the future too.

20 SATURDAY

Moon Age Day 13 • Moon Sign Aquarius

am ....

pm ....

Favours come your way again today, and you may decide that a change of scenery could cheer things up no end. You should be able to kill two birds with one stone by being willing to embark on a shopping spree or some other little adventure that would cheer you up. A more dynamic approach might help.

21 SUNDAY

Moon Age Day 14 • Moon Sign Aquarius

am ....

pm ....

Although you are probably not anywhere near as organised generally as you would wish to be right now, some hitches could come along to slow things down even more. Confidence in your own abilities is not high, all the more reason to stay well away from important issues today, concentrating instead on less demanding situations.

← *NEGATIVE TREND*							*POSITIVE TREND* →			
-5	-4	-3	-2	-1		+1	+2	+3	+4	+5
					LOVE					
					MONEY					
					LUCK					
					VITALITY					

22 MONDAY
Moon Age Day 15 • Moon Sign Pisces

am ....

pm ....

In your work you are now definitely out for a piece of the action. This means a more dominant sort of Libran, something that not everyone is able to come to terms with all that easily. Avoid pendulum swings in your nature and opt instead for your usual desire to achieve the balance that is the hallmark of your sign.

23 TUESDAY
Moon Age Day 16 • Moon Sign Pisces

am ....

pm ....

The Sun wanders into your solar twelfth house, and this means that you now embark on a period when you would be doing all that you can to clear up issues in your life that no longer serve any purpose. This is a situation that should go on for the next month or so, and the process could prove to be quite distracting.

24 WEDNESDAY
Moon Age Day 17 • Moon Sign Aries

am ....

pm ....

The arrival of the lunar low today may seem to represent a low ebb as far as you are concerned, though if you use the situation carefully, nothing could be further from the truth. Just remember that plans which are not turning out the way that you might wish should now be removed from your life as soon as possible.

25 THURSDAY
Moon Age Day 18 • Moon Sign Aries

am ....

pm ....

There won't be the number of favours coming from the direction of your colleagues and friends that you might have expected, another fact that you can blame on the present position of the Moon. In some respects you may not be all that worried about the fact since you will be in the mood to spend time on your own in any case.

26 FRIDAY
Moon Age Day 19 • Moon Sign Aries

am ....

pm ....

The atmosphere now becomes much more favourable with regard to one-to-one relationships. Today stimulates an easy and carefree attitude. There is little enough time to rest or to do those things that really take your fancy, so it is simply a matter of organising things carefully and making the most of the hours available.

27 SATURDAY
Moon Age Day 20 • Moon Sign Taurus

am ....

pm ....

What a good day for becoming more organised with regard to the practical necessities of your life and for making the most of every new opportunity that comes your way. You could fit masses into the next twenty-four hours if you really put your mind to it, and you may be in the running for some special sort of favour.

28 SUNDAY
Moon Age Day 21 • Moon Sign Taurus

am ....

pm ....

An adverse aspect between Venus and Neptune could make others 'cling' more tightly than may be strictly comfortable. There could also be some surprising events to come to terms with in a personal sense, though you should not expect these to be bad ones. Favourable trends exist with regard to new friendships if you look for them.

← NEGATIVE TREND							POSITIVE TREND →			
-5	-4	-3	-2	-1		+1	+2	+3	+4	+5
					LOVE					
					MONEY					
					LUCK					
					VITALITY					

29 MONDAY   *Moon Age Day 22 • Moon Sign Gemini*

am ....

pm ....

In a practical sense, the day should run smoothly enough, but there are certain mysteries that will need to be resolved and as a result you could well be putting on your Sherlock Holmes hat. Colleagues and even close friends make it their business to let you know when they think your attitude is wrong, that is if you want to listen.

30 TUESDAY   *Moon Age Day 23 • Moon Sign Gemini*

am ....

pm ....

A more dynamic Libran now greets the day. In conversation it's time to be putting all your cards on the table and to be making the sort of impression on those in command that could not fail to impress them. Whatever you do today is likely to bring significant results, so don't stand in the shadows.

31 WEDNESDAY   *Moon Age Day 24 • Moon Sign Gemini*

am ....

pm ....

Results come in thanks to the efforts that you have put in so far, especially in a professional sense. For some Librans it is now time to reap the benefits of hard work that has gone before and you should not hold back when it comes to deciding that the time is right to please yourself more than ever.

1 THURSDAY   *Moon Age Day 25 • Moon Sign Cancer*

am ....

pm ....

With a more retrograde attitude, you won't be quite as up to the mark today as may appear to have been the case of late. The path ahead is not as clear now as may seem to have been the case recently, though all you really need is more rest and some plans for alternatives that you can put into action at the weekend.

2 FRIDAY

Moon Age Day 26 • Moon Sign Cancer

am ....

pm ....

You won't want to be sharing all your plans with everyone. For a start you have to realise that different people have very differing points of view, not all of which fall in line with your own way of thinking. Discuss the most important of your ideas with a trusted adviser and then put them into definite action.

3 SATURDAY

Moon Age Day 27 • Moon Sign Leo

am ....

pm ....

A boost comes in terms of general optimism, no doubt fostered by the arrival of the weekend and the realisation that many of the choices today are really down to you. A weekend to enjoy any good weather that may be about and for getting yourself out into the fresh air for a change. New sporting possibilities beckon.

4 SUNDAY

Moon Age Day 28 • Moon Sign Leo

am ....

pm ....

Mercury enters your solar first house, always good news for you since it offers a mental peak and a strong alert to what is going on in your vicinity. An excellent period for all talking and for generally deciding the way that you would wish your life to go. You can also gain by chatting to almost anyone.

← NEGATIVE TREND								POSITIVE TREND →				
-5	-4	-3	-2	-1			+1	+2	+3	+4	+5
					LOVE						
					MONEY						
					LUCK						
					VITALITY						

1994

YOUR MONTH AT A GLANCE

The twelve numbered boxes represent the important areas in your life.
The key to the numbers you will find beneath the panel. A Sun above
the number indicates that opportunities are around. A Cloud below
the number, that you should be a bit defensive. Nothing above or
below and life will be pretty ordinary.

KEY

1 Strength of Personality
2 Personal Finance
3 Useful Information Gathering
4 Domestic Affairs
5 Pleasure & Romance
6 Effective Work & Health

7 One to One Relationships
8 Questioning, Thinking & Deciding
9 External Influences / Education
10 Career Aspirations
11 Teamwork Activities
12 Unconscious Impulses

SEPTEMBER HIGHS AND LOWS

Here, I show how the rhythm of the Moon will affect you this month.
Like the tide, your energies and abilities will rise and fall with its pattern. When it is above the date line, go-for-it. When it is below the
line you should be resting.

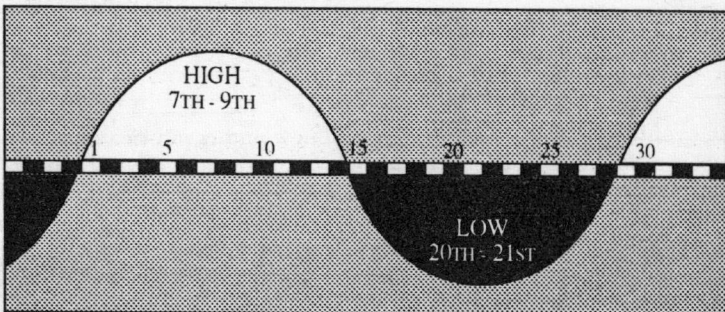

HIGH
7TH - 9TH

1   5   10   15   20   25   30

LOW
20TH - 21ST

5 MONDAY
Moon Age Day 0 • Moon Sign Virgo

am ....

pm ....

A strange sort of day with some rather obscure and unusual aspects about. What is really important is to sit down and talk all matters through as carefully as you can. Reacting too strongly to any situation would definitely be a mistake. The vague ideas of those around you are no substitute for practical common sense.

6 TUESDAY
Moon Age Day 1 • Moon Sign Virgo

am ....

pm ....

The company of other people is very important to you at the moment, so take every opportunity to brighten your social life and to make the most of all possibilities that mean a fuller and more varied life. What you don't need at present is to get yourself into a rut of any sort, which would really be restricting.

7 WEDNESDAY
Moon Age Day 2 • Moon Sign Libra

am ....

pm ....

The lunar high is almost certain to bring a lucky feel to the day, and this means that you are now more willing, almost instinctively, to take a chance of some sort. All the same, you would not be well advised to put all your money on one gamble, no matter what kind of a certainty it seems to be. Routines can be tedious.

8 THURSDAY
Moon Age Day 3 • Moon Sign Libra

am ....

pm ....

The events of today could point you in new and revolutionary directions, not to mention encouraging you to make more of your natural talents in the days to come. Arguments at home should be kept to a minimum, assuming that you have any choice in the matter. At least you do not have to join in with them.

9 FRIDAY

Moon Age Day 4 • Moon Sign Libra

am ....

pm ....

Venus, presently in your solar second house, stimulates generosity to all people with whom you associate. Further than this it could mean a significant degree of kindness coming back in your direction. Conversation is apt to be interesting, and to carry possibilities that you really hadn't thought about previously.

10 SATURDAY

Moon Age Day 5 • Moon Sign Scorpio

am ....

pm ....

Work plans need looking at carefully, and especially so in the case of Librans who do not work at the weekend. You need the distance so that you can look at things in a less fettered way and so that you can make the most of impressions that don't come along when you are in the middle of a busy working schedule.

11 SUNDAY

Moon Age Day 6 • Moon Sign Scorpio

am ....

pm ....

Finances now need some careful appraisal and it would be a mistake to spend any significant amount of money at present before you have checked that you are really getting value for your cash. You do have the ability to influence the attitudes of those who hold the purse strings, in situations where you do not.

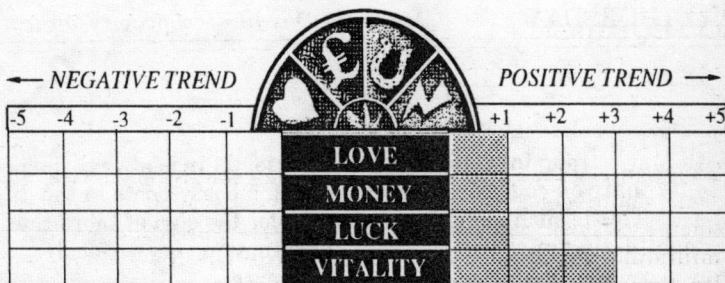

← *NEGATIVE TREND*   *POSITIVE TREND* →

-5	-4	-3	-2	-1		+1	+2	+3	+4	+5
					LOVE					
					MONEY					
					LUCK					
					VITALITY					

12 MONDAY
Moon Age Day 7 • Moon Sign Sagittarius

am ....

pm ....

Any sort of professional pressure that you may have felt to be placed upon you now appears to be lifting. The influence that you may have recognised with others yesterday is, if anything, increased now. This is a really good time to go out and ask for what you want. You could be surprised at the results.

13 TUESDAY
Moon Age Day 8 • Moon Sign Sagittarius

am ....

pm ....

Behind closed doors at least you should recognise the arrival of a peaceful and serene atmosphere, even if life out on the the street is far more hectic. Perhaps you should take a look at family expenditure in order to see what you can do to cut back a little, if only for the next week or two.

14 WEDNESDAY
Moon Age Day 9 • Moon Sign Capricorn

am ....

pm ....

Your mind is inclined to look to the past today, rather than towards what you may see as a rather uncertain future. In fact there is no reason at all to be pessimistic, it's simply the way that your mind is working at present. Buried tensions should be brought to the surface and dealt with by subjecting them to common-sense.

15 THURSDAY
Moon Age Day 10 • Moon Sign Capricorn

am ....

pm ....

With Mars strong in your solar tenth house, there is always the possibility that you could be accused of being a bossy-boots in the days ahead. This is such a strange departure for the sign of Libra that it is doubtful that anyone would take the situation very seriously. The reason could be a continued lack of confidence.

16 FRIDAY
Moon Age Day 11 • Moon Sign Aquarius

am ....

pm ....

There are thrilling times in the offing for some Librans, and whether
or not you are one of them depends in part on your ability to cast
your mind forward in order to make the most of travel opportunities.
This should be a good day from a social point-of-view, and one on
which you need to ring the changes in friendships a little.

17 SATURDAY
Moon Age Day 12 • Moon Sign Aquarius

am ....

pm ....

Progress should now be fairly obvious in your life, even if it is of the
slow and steady kind. You should notice certain subtle signs of
improvement financially, allowing more flexibility, greater diversity
and significant optimism. Creating space for yourself to grow is an
important part of the weekend.

18 SUNDAY
Moon Age Day 13 • Moon Sign Pisces

am ....

pm ....

There is no lack of co-operation, one of the facts that ought to make
today go reasonably smoothly for most of you. This should not be a
time for trying to catch up with all outstanding jobs however and
you would be well advised to think about how you can get a little
more free time than seems to be likely.

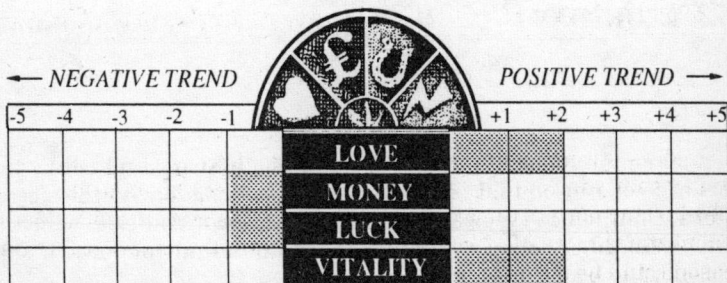

← NEGATIVE TREND　　　　　　*POSITIVE TREND →*

-5	-4	-3	-2	-1			+1	+2	+3	+4	+5
					LOVE						
					MONEY						
					LUCK						
					VITALITY						

19 MONDAY
Moon Age Day 14 • Moon Sign Pisces

am ....

pm ....

Minor financial gains could be on the way, together with a show of generosity from others, and especially your partner if you have one. At the same time you should keep your eye out for unexpected financial obligations or at the very least ones that you had forgotten about.

20 TUESDAY
Moon Age Day 15 • Moon Sign Pisces

am ....

pm ....

Although you do your best to shine in social situations, the truth of the matter is that you are not working on full-power today, all the more reason to slow things down a little and not to rush anything at all. In a practical sense you can get things done rather efficiently, as long as you do not rush your fences.

21 WEDNESDAY
Moon Age Day 16 • Moon Sign Aries

am ....

pm ....

If the last day or so has felt a little like hard work, you can probably blame the lunar low, which is still around now. The best way to deal with this situation is simply to register the fact and then to forget about it. A slight lack of energy merely means that you must take things more steadily.

22 THURSDAY
Moon Age Day 17 • Moon Sign Aries

am ....

pm ....

You make the greatest gains today by going it alone, and not by the sort of co-operation that is more normally associated with the sign of Libra. Confidence is low, especially in your own abilities, which is why you need to gather every remaining ounce that you have, if only to fool other people for a day or two.

23 FRIDAY
Moon Age Day 18 • Moon Sign Taurus

am ....

pm ....

The Sun enters your solar first house, at a time when you may feel yourself to be in need of a boost of some sort. This increases your sense of personal gain in life and also offers new incentives on a number of levels. A more powerful Libran is on display and there is planning to undertake for the weekend.

24 SATURDAY
Moon Age Day 19 • Moon Sign Taurus

am ....

pm ....

Not a day to be looking back. Nearly all favourable planetary incentives point you towards the future, and the very real possibilities that lie in store for you. Intimate relationships are well starred, and this fact could mean extra romance in the lives of some. For more settled Librans it spells a better understanding.

25 SUNDAY
Moon Age Day 20 • Moon Sign Taurus

am ....

pm ....

There was rarely a better time than this for asking people to help you, or for making requests that you may normally shy away from. Most people you come across should be impressed with your decisive manner and the way in which you are willing to roll up your sleeves and help someone else out of a jam.

← *NEGATIVE TREND*   *POSITIVE TREND* →

-5	-4	-3	-2	-1		+1	+2	+3	+4	+5
					LOVE					
					MONEY					
					LUCK					
					VITALITY					

26 MONDAY
Moon Age Day 21 • Moon Sign Gemini

am ....

pm ....

You need more change and diversity than the average September Monday is apt to provide, all the more reason to implement a few subtle alterations at least. Any opportunity for travel, either now, or even in the planning stage, should be grasped firmly with both hands. Renewed optimism is a hall-mark of the present period.

27 TUESDAY
Moon Age Day 22 • Moon Sign Gemini

am ....

pm ....

Mercury enters your solar second house and with it come new ideas for improving your income. You are now able to plan more effectively than has been the case for a while and can hold a number of different ideas in your head. What might be more of a problem is knowing how to get ideas off the ground.

28 WEDNESDAY
Moon Age Day 23 • Moon Sign Cancer

am ....

pm ....

A combination of Venus and Jupiter now brings the practical ability to do some of the things that have been on your mind in the recent past. Work towards all your goals slowly and steadily, making certain that you know what is expected of you on the way. You can ask for more in the way of support from friends.

29 THURSDAY
Moon Age Day 24 • Moon Sign Cancer

am ....

pm ....

Hasty decisions are for the birds today, in fact almost any kind of major change in your life can wait for a while. Others are asking you to get your practical head on to offer them the sort of advice that you excel at offering. It's certain that you will not let down the many people who presently rely on you.

30 FRIDAY

Moon Age Day 25 • Moon Sign Cancer

am ....

pm ....

Aspects of your love-life demonstrate your present cheerful attitude, and your ability to make the best out of almost any situation that comes your way. In a professional sense, it's business as usual, though this would not be a good time for allowing yourself to be forced down avenues that you don't care for the look of.

1 SATURDAY

Moon Age Day 26 • Moon Sign Leo

am ....

pm ....

Suddenly it appears that 'image' is all-important. The way that you behave in public seems to be far more important than would have been the case only a few days ago and the more flamboyant aspects of your nature rise to the surface. You can make a real success of almost anything that you choose to undertake.

2 SUNDAY

Moon Age Day 27 • Moon Sign Leo

am ....

pm ....

Though there are a wealth of people who would try to talk you into situations that you are not too keen on, both your presence of mind and your resilience are important factors, so you would not be easily fooled by anyone at all. Emotional relationships take on a new feel and romance fills the air for the next few days.

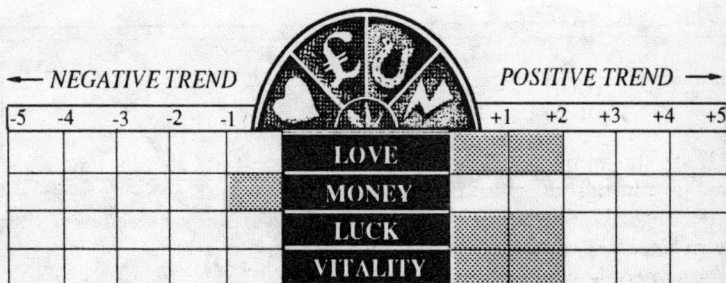

← NEGATIVE TREND								POSITIVE TREND →		
-5	-4	-3	-2	-1		+1	+2	+3	+4	+5
					LOVE					
					MONEY					
					LUCK					
					VITALITY					

OCTOBER

1994

YOUR MONTH AT A GLANCE

The twelve numbered boxes represent the important areas in your life.
The key to the numbers you will find beneath the panel. A Sun above
the number indicates that opportunities are around. A Cloud below
the number, that you should be a bit defensive. Nothing above or
below and life will be pretty ordinary.

1	2	3	4	5	6	7	8	9	10	11	12

KEY

1 Strength of Personality
2 Personal Finance
3 Useful Information Gathering
4 Domestic Affairs
5 Pleasure & Romance
6 Effective Work & Health

7 One to One Relationships
8 Questioning, Thinking & Deciding
9 External Influences / Education
10 Career Aspirations
11 Teamwork Activities
12 Unconscious Impulses

OCTOBER HIGHS AND LOWS

Here, I show how the rhythm of the Moon will affect you this month.
Like the tide, your energies and abilities will rise and fall with its pattern. When it is above the date line, go-for-it. When it is below the
line you should be resting.

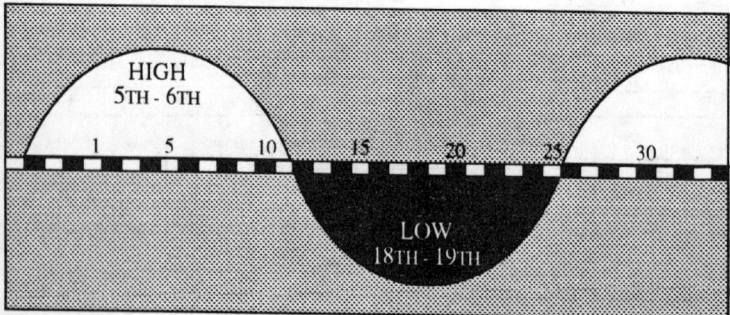

HIGH
5TH - 6TH

1   5   10   15   20   25   30

LOW
18TH - 19TH

3 MONDAY

Moon Age Day 28 • Moon Sign Virgo

am ....

pm ....

The practical details of your everyday life are easy to deal with at the start of this working week. For most Librans there is a boost to health associations and the ability to feel that life is generally going your way. Unfinished business that needs to be dealt with fairly quickly should be tackled now.

4 TUESDAY

Moon Age Day 29 • Moon Sign Virgo

am ....

pm ....

Along comes the lunar high, and you should be on sparkling form once again. Discussions that are undertaken today show how much you are bearing in mind the opinions of all those people who have meant so much to you in the recent past. All the same, it is your own opinions that really count for now.

5 WEDNESDAY

Moon Age Day 0 • Moon Sign Libra

am ....

pm ....

Emotional rewards come from the direction of your love life, and especially so in the case of Librans who have been actively seeking a new relationship. For the more settled amongst you there is a change in attitude that you should find to be especially useful. Your requests to others bring valuable help.

6 THURSDAY

Moon Age Day 1 • Moon Sign Libra

am ....

pm ....

It is still worth sticking your neck out and asking for what you want of others. Even if you feel that some of your requests are a little over the top, the people with whom you deal could turn out to be more accommodating than you would imagine. There is fun to be had, especially if you are willing to look for it.

7 FRIDAY

Moon Age Day 2 • Moon Sign Scorpio

am ....

pm ....

New friendships now become possible, with a host of new relation-ships on the way and contacts with people from all walks of life. The range of experience that this brings in turns out to be rather valu-able further down the line. Not a period for taking your own nature or influence for granted.

8 SATURDAY

Moon Age Day 3 • Moon Sign Scorpio

am ....

pm ....

In social situations you are now more than willing to tell others the way you feel about almost anything. This is fine as long as you are careful not to take offence. It's true that your ideas all have some merit, but are you being your usual tactful self? It's what you are most liked and respected for.

9 SUNDAY

Moon Age Day 4 • Moon Sign Sagittarius

am ....

pm ....

The simple pleasures of life really appeal to you at present, which may be part of the reason that you are so willing to spend time on your own, away from the rat-race and the many needs that the rest of the world seems to have of you. A little dissatisfaction can be expected at present, but should not be allowed to grow.

← NEGATIVE TREND						POSITIVE TREND →				
-5	-4	-3	-2	-1		+1	+2	+3	+4	+5
					LOVE					
					MONEY					
					LUCK					
					VITALITY					

10 MONDAY
Moon Age Day 5 • Moon Sign Sagittarius

am ....

pm ....

A rather tense aspect between the Sun and Saturn is inclined to make you take others for granted much more than would normally be the case. This could mean that one or two people are not as helpful in return. A time to take time out to please yourself, and for doing what you know to be right in a personal or romantic sense.

11 TUESDAY
Moon Age Day 6 • Moon Sign Capricorn

am ....

pm ....

You can do much now to reduce the worries of people you care about, even on those occasions when you don't consider that they have anything to worry about. This would be a good time to encourage others to do what is right, though you do realise that you lack the farsightedness that sometimes attends your nature.

12 WEDNESDAY
Moon Age Day 7 • Moon Sign Capricorn

am ....

pm ....

In discussions or arguments, it is too easy to feel that others are getting the better of you, which is why you need to express your point-of-view as forcefully as your easy-going nature allows. Most important of all, let people know how you really feel, freed from the fetters of convention.

13 THURSDAY
Moon Age Day 8 • Moon Sign Aquarius

am ....

pm ....

Romantic possibilities bring out the child in you, an aspect of the Libran nature that is never very far from the surface in any case. A very generous quality comes to your life now, which is fine just as long as you have the financial clout to back it up. There are other ways of showing how much you care.

14 FRIDAY
Moon Age Day 9 • Moon Sign Aquarius

am ....

pm ....

The present position of Neptune, and its association with other planets, can make you feel very safe and secure at present. However, it is a double-edged sword because it can encourage you to become quite bored with routines. The best course of action would be to vary things and not to allow yourself too much spare time.

15 SATURDAY
Moon Age Day 10 • Moon Sign Pisces

am ....

pm ....

It's business as usual on the home-front, with little to set the weekend apart unless you put in the effort and do something about it yourself. Despite recent progress you can easily become dissatisfied with your life, which would not be exactly fair considering the progress of the last few weeks. Stay away from routines.

16 SUNDAY
Moon Age Day 11 • Moon Sign Pisces

am ....

pm ....

You need change and diversity now, because too much sticking around the house can bring out the worst in you, and in the people you care about the most. New friendships can be worked on, as well as gaining strength from groups or organisations that you have recently been cultivating. Conflict should be avoided.

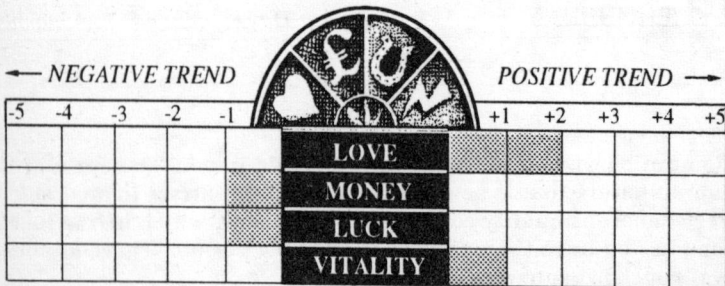

NEGATIVE TREND							POSITIVE TREND			
-5	-4	-3	-2	-1			+1	+2	+3	+4	+5
LOVE										
MONEY										
LUCK										
VITALITY										

17 MONDAY

Moon Age Day 12 • Moon Sign Pisces

am ....

pm ....

The lunar low is almost certainly going to bring a lull in affairs, and especially so if you try to do anything at a break-neck pace. The more you are willing to accommodate a quieter time by using it wisely, the better things should turn out for you. Don't turn down advice that is on offer later in the day.

18 TUESDAY

Moon Age Day 13 • Moon Sign Aries

am ....

pm ....

Minor frustrations can be expected, though these should not be allowed to interfere with a period that has much going for it in other ways. Friends are helpful and understanding, whilst relatives are also in a position to help you out. Renewed confidence can be a goal to work towards, even if it is lacking now.

19 WEDNESDAY

Moon Age Day 14 • Moon Sign Aries

am ....

pm ....

A heavy work-load is something that you will want to avoid taking on if you possibly can. This is a time for companionship and for making the most of new friendships, not to mention recent improvements in your personal life. Problems, where they exist, should be dealt with carefully and with much humour.

20 THURSDAY

Moon Age Day 15 • Moon Sign Taurus

am ....

pm ....

Mercury in your solar first house means that the pace of your everyday life is certain to quicken, the more so with the Moon now racing away from your opposite sign. Radical new ideas pop in and out of your head, and it feels as if you somehow have to make up for lost time. Do your best to be consistent.

21 FRIDAY
Moon Age Day 16 • Moon Sign Taurus

am ....

pm ....

You are very unlikely to back down if you feel yourself to be
threatened in friendships today. The brave side of Libra makes you
willing to stand your ground, even with people you know to be
influential. The chances are that you will be respected for your
views in the end, so it's worth being just a little insistent.

22 SATURDAY
Moon Age Day 17 • Moon Sign Taurus

am ....

pm ....

Don't expect more from others than they seem naturally willing to
offer. Your tolerance level is not what it might be, or what it usually
is. All the same, you should be willing to allow those around you the
right to hold their own views, even if they differ radically from your
own. Money matters need some discussing.

23 SUNDAY
Moon Age Day 18 • Moon Sign Gemini

am ....

pm ....

The Sun now wanders into your solar second house, lifting some of
the financial restrictions that have stood around you for some time.
You can be rather undecided in some topics, though this will not
prevent you from making the most of what the days ahead have to
offer you. Some Librans will be thinking about new adventures
now.

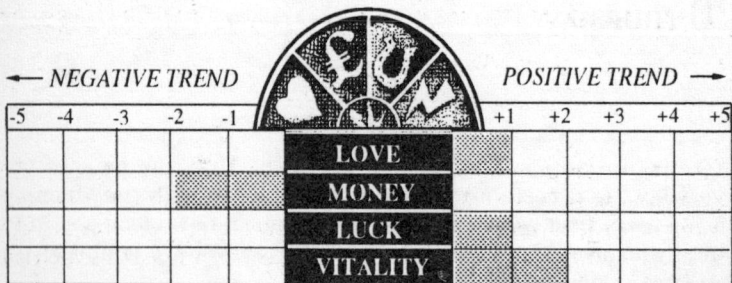

← NEGATIVE TREND						POSITIVE TREND →				
-5	-4	-3	-2	-1		+1	+2	+3	+4	+5
LOVE										
MONEY										
LUCK										
VITALITY										

24 MONDAY
Moon Age Day 19 • Moon Sign Gemini

am ....

pm ....

If discussions, or heaven forbid, arguments come along today, it should be quite easy for you to get the better of others. A far more forceful Libran greets the start of a new working week, even if this comes as something of a shock to certain people in your vicinity. The lighter side of life should be cultivated too.

25 TUESDAY
Moon Age Day 20 • Moon Sign Cancer

am ....

pm ....

Financial and property dealings can come to your aid in the days ahead, especially if things have been a little quiet in this sphere of your life for some time now. Fluctuations now tend to stabilise, which also holds good in a relationship sense, since you are more consistent in your general approach to them.

26 WEDNESDAY
Moon Age Day 21 • Moon Sign Cancer

am ....

pm ....

People with whom you deal are pleased, not only with your attitude to life but also on account of your ability to plan well ahead. This could be the best period of the month to make a good impression, and brings benefits that you neither expected or desired. You tend to be rather non-materialistic at present.

27 THURSDAY
Moon Age Day 22 • Moon Sign Cancer

am ....

pm ....

Don't let disagreements over minor issues get to you. There is far too much to keep you occupied at present to allow yourself to be held back by details of any sort, so do what you can to take life in your stride, spreading your energy carefully, though not too much so. Financial luck should improve noticeably.

28 FRIDAY

Moon Age Day 23 • Moon Sign Leo

am ....

pm ....

Not a good time for allowing yourself to become complacent about anything at all. You don't lack concentration, or the ability to make much of your opportunities, though you could find that you take situations so much for granted that you are not in a position to change direction if you have to.

29 SATURDAY

Moon Age Day 24 • Moon Sign Leo

am ....

pm ....

There could be difficulties on a personal level that could be put down in part to muddled thinking. It is important to be precise in your estimations and not to take on more than you know you can success- fully cope with in terms of extra responsibility. A good time for a family-motivated weekend.

30 SUNDAY

Moon Age Day 25 • Moon Sign Virgo

am ....

pm ....

Eager to form fresh social contacts, you should be more than willing to put yourself about a little today. This would not be a good time for thinking too much about the details of your life, more a period for getting stuck into the host of social possibilities that exist. Make the most of friendships.

◄— NEGATIVE TREND　　　　*POSITIVE TREND —►*

-5	-4	-3	-2	-1			+1	+2	+3	+4	+5
					LOVE						
					MONEY						
					LUCK						
					VITALITY						

31 MONDAY
Moon Age Day 26 • Moon Sign Virgo

am ....

pm ....

It would be very easy today to allow yourself to be led down blind alleys, especially in a career sense. Fortunately you do have your sensible head on at present and can be relied upon to look at things carefully. You may also be called upon to lend a hand with friends who need your support.

1 TUESDAY
Moon Age Day 27 • Moon Sign Libra

am ....

pm ....

With even greater confidence comes the knowledge that you are working slowly but surely towards your objectives. The lunar high brings a lucky streak into your life, made all the more useful by your ability to be in the right place at the right time. Rewards do not always come from the most likely of directions at present.

2 WEDNESDAY
Moon Age Day 28 • Moon Sign Libra

am ....

pm ....

Much positive progress now seems likely. Keep an open mind and do not allow your good-nature to be taken for granted, especially not considering that you have the ability and the need to feather your own nest for once. New relationships begin to take on a greater significance in your life, and need to be nurtured.

3 THURSDAY
Moon Age Day 0 • Moon Sign Scorpio

am ....

pm ....

The creative plans of others can be taken one step further when you come to putting your thinking cap on at the moment. It isn't that you would be seeking to dupe anyone, merely that you are able to contribute your ideas and to co-operate in a way that no sign understands better than yourself does.

4 FRIDAY
Moon Age Day 1• Moon Sign Scorpio

am ....

pm ....

The need for some limited financial restraint could cause you to stop and think twice about some of the more important expenses in your life. Perhaps you could do a little reorganising, in which case you should be able to make cash go further than it does right now. Away from money, new incentives appear at work.

5 SATURDAY
Moon Age Day 2 • Moon Sign Sagittarius

am ....

pm ....

What a splendid weekend this should be for making the most of a much enlivened social scene. You are certainly in the limelight when it comes to group encounters and can also gain through mixing with friends who you don't really see all that often, but who are nevertheless important in the mainstream of your life.

6 SUNDAY
Moon Age Day 3 • Moon Sign Sagittarius

am ....

pm ....

There is a definite emphasis on taking life more steadily than has been the case in the recent past. Look carefully at all possible options before you decide to commit yourself to any one. Confidence could seem to be lacking early in the day but does improve in the fullness of time. Patience is also a little low.

← NEGATIVE TREND						POSITIVE TREND →				
-5	-4	-3	-2	-1		+1	+2	+3	+4	+5
					LOVE					
					MONEY					
					LUCK					
					VITALITY					

1994

YOUR MONTH AT A GLANCE

The twelve numbered boxes represent the important areas in your life. The key to the numbers you will find beneath the panel. A Sun above the number indicates that opportunities are around. A Cloud below the number, that you should be a bit defensive. Nothing above or below and life will be pretty ordinary.

KEY	
1 Strength of Personality	7 One to One Relationships
2 Personal Finance	8 Questioning, Thinking & Deciding
3 Useful Information Gathering	9 External Influences / Education
4 Domestic Affairs	10 Career Aspirations
5 Pleasure & Romance	11 Teamwork Activities
6 Effective Work & Health	12 Unconscious Impulses

NOVEMBER HIGHS AND LOWS

Here, I show how the rhythm of the Moon will affect you this month. Like the tide, your energies and abilities will rise and fall with its pattern. When it is above the date line, go-for-it. When it is below the line you should be resting.

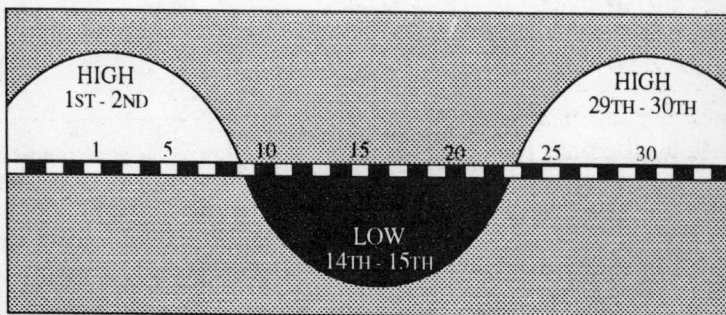

HIGH
1ST - 2ND

HIGH
29TH - 30TH

LOW
14TH - 15TH

7 MONDAY
Moon Age Day 4 • Moon Sign Capricorn

am ....

pm ....

Some restlessness is almost inevitable at first today, though this should not stay around for very long. The secret is to keep yourself fully occupied. Family concerns are of the greatest importance just now and you may turn your attention towards helping someone close to you fulfil a personal objective.

8 TUESDAY
Moon Age Day 5 • Moon Sign Capricorn

am ....

pm ....

You should be anxious to see some fairly rapid progress in your life now and will be able to get ahead as a result of improved communication skills and better powers of persuasion. Not every discussion can be turned to your advantage however and tact is an important commodity in your dealings with others.

9 WEDNESDAY
Moon Age Day 6 • Moon Sign Aquarius

am ....

pm ....

Some people seem to be making mountains out of molehills today, whilst you do your best to calm things down generally. Not everyone in your circle can be trusted at present, even if one or two surprising people cross your path. It might be worth listening to what they have to say.

10 THURSDAY
Moon Age Day 7 • Moon Sign Aquarius

am ....

pm ....

Look to situations from the past to guide you down the path towards professional successes today. Those Librans who may be out of work could find new opportunities beckoning fairly soon. Gains can be made as a result of improved powers of communication and the ability to put what you know to good use.

11 FRIDAY
Moon Age Day 8 • Moon Sign Aquarius

am ....

pm ....

Things may not work out as well or as quickly as you would wish,
no matter how good the day turns out to be. The simple fact is that
you want to rush your fences in just about everything. In reality you
could do with sitting back and taking life steadily, though this is
something you are unwilling to do.

12 SATURDAY
Moon Age Day 9 • Moon Sign Pisces

am ....

pm ....

Things that are said on the spur of the moment are not at all easy to
take back, all the more reason to be a little cautious this weekend
before you commit yourself. It isn't that you mean to give offence,
and there are some very sensitive types about. Try to help friends
out of the doldrums.

13 SUNDAY
Moon Age Day 10 • Moon Sign Pisces

am ....

pm ....

A favourable combination of Mercury and Venus brings a more hopeful and constructive phase into your life than you might feel the last
week has been able to offer. There is great encouragement about,
probably from the directions of relatives as well as friends. Think
about new social possibilities during the next few days.

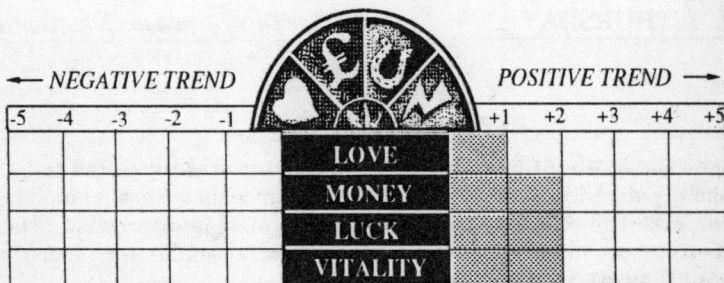

← NEGATIVE TREND								POSITIVE TREND →				
-5	-4	-3	-2	-1			+1	+2	+3	+4	+5
					LOVE						
					MONEY						
					LUCK						
					VITALITY						

14 MONDAY
Moon Age Day 11 • Moon Sign Aries

am ....

pm ....

The arrival of the Moon in the sign of Aries will not do much to lift your spirits today, but as long as you are willing to take a sideways look at certain situations this could turn out to be a good day all the same. Try to avoid becoming bogged down with routines and look on the bright side of life.

15 TUESDAY
Moon Age Day 12 • Moon Sign Aries

am ....

pm ....

The expectations of friends could place strains on you unless you let them know that you need some rest yourself. Meanwhile your social life will take on a completely new feel, with new friendships likely to emerge and people generally doing what they can to make things a little easier for you.

16 WEDNESDAY
Moon Age Day 13 • Moon Sign Aries

am ....

pm ....

A greater degree of personal satisfaction should be coming your way today, at a time when life generally is looking brighter. The path towards your personal ambitions is now more clearly marked and you are able to make the most of opportunities that you may not have thought about previously.

17 THURSDAY
Moon Age Day 14 • Moon Sign Taurus

am ....

pm ....

It is the more intimate side of relationships that you find to be of the greatest importance now and you can come to terms much better with the real love that surrounds you. Listen to what others have to say about both practical and social matters, chances are that they are talking a great deal of sense.

18 FRIDAY
Moon Age Day 15 • Moon Sign Taurus

am ....

pm ....

Some fairly significant monetary gains come your way now and you should be in a position to strike while the iron is hot in all practical matters. You tend to be in the good books of others, and could make gains as a result of the efforts of influential types, who can be persuaded to work on your behalf.

19 SATURDAY
Moon Age Day 16 • Moon Sign Gemini

am ....

pm ....

Not everyone who you meet today turns out to be what they appear at first sight, all the more reason to look carefully and not to take any situation at face value. Plan now for journeys later, but don't turn down the chance of getting away from things in the immediate future if opportunities present themselves.

20 SUNDAY
Moon Age Day 17 • Moon Sign Gemini

am ....

pm ....

Casual social acquaintances tend to win out over more established friendships now. You are certainly not in the mood to take life too seriously and should be able to find reasons to laugh now. Demands are made of you that could be rather difficult to fulfil, and this means looking for compromises.

← *NEGATIVE TREND*   *POSITIVE TREND* →

-5	-4	-3	-2	-1		+1	+2	+3	+4	+5
					LOVE					
					MONEY					
					LUCK					
					VITALITY					

21 MONDAY
Moon Age Day 18 • Moon Sign Gemini

am ....

pm ....

Positive news from colleagues means a shot in the arm for ambitions, at the start of what could turn out to be a very positive working week. In both a professional and a personal sense you should find that you are in the limelight, and will be able to bring all manner of people round to your particular point of view.

22 TUESDAY
Moon Age Day 19 • Moon Sign Cancer

am ....

pm ....

As the Sun enters your solar third house, so you find that your social life begins to take on a new dimension. In conversation you tend to be impressive and more forthright than could usually be said to be the case for the sign of Libra. Of course, not everyone agrees with your point of view but you are very persuasive.

23 WEDNESDAY
Moon Age Day 20 • Moon Sign Cancer

am ....

pm ....

Because Venus is now strong in your solar second house, you should not be too surprised to find that your desire nature is being stimulated. This could mean looking carefully at spending, because you are in the mood to fritter away your resources without making certain that you are getting value for money.

24 THURSDAY
Moon Age Day 21 • Moon Sign Leo

am ....

pm ....

There is a moment to watch and a second when positive action can really pay off. Knowing the difference between the two could be very important today. There are significant gains to be made and plenty of people who would be willing to give you a helping hand, if you stop still long enough to recognise the fact!

25 FRIDAY
Moon Age Day 22 • Moon Sign Leo

am ....

pm ....

Although you will be doing your best to please others, don't be too surprised if your efforts fail in some way. In any case you can only do so much and do need to take account of the fact that what you think is good for them may not match their own estimation. A happy atmosphere prevails generally however.

26 SATURDAY
Moon Age Day 23 • Moon Sign Leo

am ....

pm ....

Not everything that you have to say today will go down all that well with the people who form a part of your social life. Perhaps you are deliberately setting out to create shock-waves, or it could be simply that your views sound radical when viewed from the very different points of perspective that you come across.

27 SUNDAY
Moon Age Day 24 • Moon Sign Virgo

am ....

pm ....

Time spend alone at present could not be said to be wasted. This is especially true when it comes to planning next moves in a professional sense, but don't spend all your time thinking exclusively about work. There are new options in a social sense, plus the chance to mix with like-minded individuals.

← *NEGATIVE TREND*   *POSITIVE TREND* →

-5	-4	-3	-2	-1		+1	+2	+3	+4	+5
					LOVE					
					MONEY					
					LUCK					
					VITALITY					

28 MONDAY
Moon Age Day 25 • Moon Sign Virgo

am ....

pm ....

If you have to take a chance of any sort, now is the best time of all for doing so. The Moon returns to your own sign today, sharpening your intellect and making it difficult for others to pull the wool over your eyes in any situation. There is greater energy at your disposal and a willingness to form partnerships.

29 TUESDAY
Moon Age Day 26 • Moon Sign Libra

am ....

pm ....

A very good day to get plans off the ground and for building on new relationships. There is a lucky phase about, and this has a bearing on most spheres of your life. Look out for new chances to make a favourable impression, people are watching you very closely at present and should be pleased to help out.

30 WEDNESDAY
Moon Age Day 27 • Moon Sign Libra

am ....

pm ....

News and views form an important part of the day. With Mercury now in your solar third house, communication skills rise to the surface, becoming much more important in terms of getting what you want from life. The only real potential problem comes from a tendency to scatter your energies a little.

1 THURSDAY
Moon Age Day 28 • Moon Sign Scorpio

am ....

pm ....

Although you can be tempted at the start of December to take shortcuts to personal growth and success, chances are that your commonsense and patience will win out in the end. Major changes are in the offing, and you need to put yourself in the right place at the right time to get the most out of them.

2 FRIDAY

Moon Age Day 29 • Moon Sign Scorpio

am ....

pm ....

Some Librans will see this as being a red-letter day, and especially so in terms of personal success. A competitive edge is evident in professional matters and those around you would be less likely to cross swords with you now than would usually be the case. Don't ignore favourable social trends.

3 SATURDAY

Moon Age Day 0 • Moon Sign Sagittarius

am ....

pm ....

With a much occupied third house, you really do find that the best way to deal with any situation is to keep talking. Comfort and security don't mean as much to you now as they may have done a while ago, though you are still not willing to cut certain ties that you recognise as being restrictive.

4 SUNDAY

Moon Age Day 1 • Moon Sign Sagittarius

am ....

pm ....

Although your judgement is still very sound, there is a distinct possibility that you will be taking a back seat where decision making is concerned. Changes occur on the home front, and this leads to a more interactive sort of day with regard to relationships. Relatives create a little confusion for you.

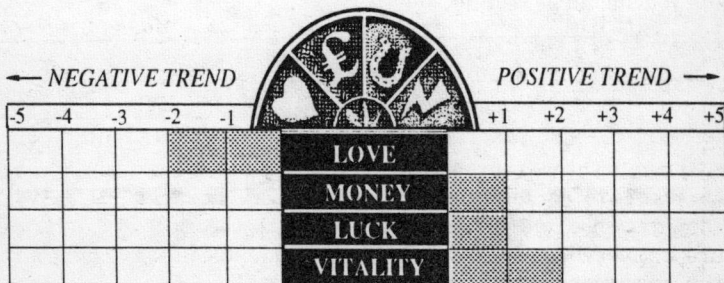

← *NEGATIVE TREND*   *POSITIVE TREND* →

-5	-4	-3	-2	-1		+1	+2	+3	+4	+5
					LOVE					
					MONEY					
					LUCK					
					VITALITY					

DECEMBER

1994

YOUR MONTH AT A GLANCE

The twelve numbered boxes represent the important areas in your life. The key to the numbers you will find beneath the panel. A Sun above the number indicates that opportunities are around. A Cloud below the number, that you should be a bit defensive. Nothing above or below and life will be pretty ordinary.

KEY

1 Strength of Personality	7 One to One Relationships
2 Personal Finance	8 Questioning, Thinking & Deciding
3 Useful Information Gathering	9 External Influences / Education
4 Domestic Affairs	10 Career Aspirations
5 Pleasure & Romance	11 Teamwork Activities
6 Effective Work & Health	12 Unconscious Impulses

DECEMBER HIGHS AND LOWS

Here, I show how the rhythm of the Moon will affect you this month. Like the tide, your energies and abilities will rise and fall with its pattern. When it is above the date line, go-for-it. When it is below the line you should be resting.

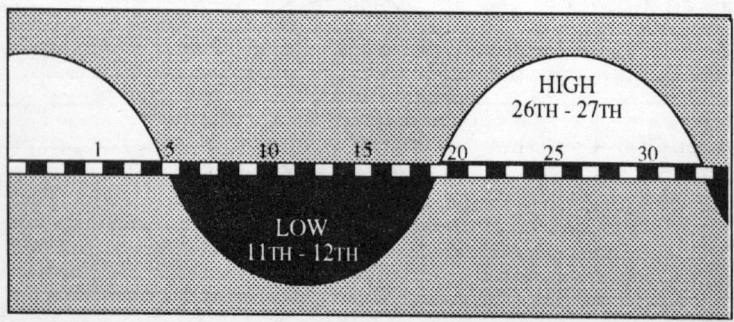

HIGH
26TH - 27TH

LOW
11TH - 12TH

5 MONDAY
Moon Age Day 2 • Moon Sign Capricorn

am ....

pm ....

Though you may consider that the actions you take today are in the best interests of others too, you should not be too surprised to discover that they meet some resistance all the same. The problem is that you think everyone else has a mind that works more or less the same as yours does and this simply is not true.

6 TUESDAY
Moon Age Day 3 • Moon Sign Capricorn

am ....

pm ....

A good day for letting your hair down and for simply being yourself. Look towards romantic possibilities and also towards spending time in places of amusement. Strangers tend to pay you a certain amount of attention, which may not be too surprising, bearing in mind your present level of magnetism.

7 WEDNESDAY
Moon Age Day 4 • Moon Sign Aquarius

am ....

pm ....

Relationships have much to offer at present and can be especially fulfilling. You may not be a lover of the middle of the week as a rule, though this one has much to offer when it comes to finding you on the road to personal progress. Some Librans may be just a little too concerned with keeping up appearances.

8 THURSDAY
Moon Age Day 5 • Moon Sign Aquarius

am ....

pm ....

Despite the effort that you are putting into life at present, and the ability that you have to make situations turn to your advantage, you could be just a little too pushy for your own good. At least you should come to terms with the physical limitations that life places upon you and get some rest as a result.

9 FRIDAY
Moon Age Day 6 • Moon Sign Pisces

am ....

pm ....

A newer, brighter and more positive phase comes along with regard
to your social and personal life. Positive thinking is much to the
fore, an important commodity when it comes to making new plans
and then putting them into action. False optimism is your only
potential adversary at the present time.

10 SATURDAY
Moon Age Day 7 • Moon Sign Pisces

am ....

pm ....

Although those in your vicinity have your best interests at heart this
might not appear to be the case at first. A good time for organising
practical matters and for getting jobs from the past out of the way
once and for all. You should be happy enough to go with the flow in
terms of social possibilities.

11 SUNDAY
Moon Age Day 8 • Moon Sign Aries

am ....

pm ....

There is good reason for the sudden fairly quiet spell that settles in
on you today. The fact is that with the Moon now in your opposite
sign and a general relaxation in your social life, you will have the
time to rest and reflect, even if this may not be exactly what you had
in mind for this December Sunday.

← *NEGATIVE TREND*   *POSITIVE TREND* →

-5	-4	-3	-2	-1		+1	+2	+3	+4	+5
					LOVE					
					MONEY					
					LUCK					
					VITALITY					

12 MONDAY
Moon Age Day 9 • Moon Sign Aries

am ....

pm ....

Although things may still be a little quiet generally, you are well able to put your plans into action before today is out. It could appear that certain situations turn to your advantage, even without you having to put in much effort. Confidence is stable, and all potential gains are worth a second look.

13 TUESDAY
Moon Age Day 10 • Moon Sign Aries

am ....

pm ....

Impetuous actions on your part today could lead to little mishaps, partly because of the position of Mars in your solar twelfth house. Most of these situations are avoidable with just a little care on your part. There is a lack of personal influence about early in the day, make up for it by being cheerful.

14 WEDNESDAY
Moon Age Day 11 • Moon Sign Taurus

am ....

pm ....

Because you are very innovative at present, and also on account of your own capacity for making the most out of situations, others are really listening to what you have to say. Your curiosity is stimulated by just about everything that you come across and that means an interesting, even exciting remainder to the week.

15 THURSDAY
Moon Age Day 12 • Moon Sign Taurus

am ....

pm ....

Financial decisions should be thought through quite carefully at present, since it would be too easy at present to stretch yourself too much. Changes in direction are more or less inevitable, though these should not be too radical at first. Give at least half an eye to the impending festive season.

179

16 FRIDAY
Moon Age Day 13 • Moon Sign Gemini

am ....

pm ....

Your opinions do not match those of the people you have to rely on today and it might be best to keep them to yourself, rather than giving offence that is not necessary. Travel matters could prove to be rather problematic and as a result you may decide to stay close to home if you have the chance to do so.

17 SATURDAY
Moon Age Day 14 • Moon Sign Gemini

am ....

pm ....

It isn't often that your sign could be accused of being arrogant, but the charge could be levelled at you right now. The difficulty seems to be that you are very anxious to express an opinion on almost any topic at present, and you may not be bearing in mind the fact that others have very different ideas.

18 SUNDAY
Moon Age Day 15 • Moon Sign Gemini

am ....

pm ....

Old ideas can be turned to your advantage with regard to new situations. This is where the hand of experience comes in rather useful, something that is often evident in the lives of wise old Libra. Now more casual in your approach, you are much less likely to come up against opposition of any sort.

← *NEGATIVE TREND*　　　　　*POSITIVE TREND* →

-5	-4	-3	-2	-1			+1	+2	+3	+4	+5
					LOVE						
					MONEY						
					LUCK						
					VITALITY						

19 MONDAY

Moon Age Day 16 • Moon Sign Cancer

am ....

pm ....

Mercury enters your solar fourth house, making your home the centre of some significant activity. Perhaps the preparations for Christmas are now in full swing and you are doing all that you can to put the finishing touches to plans. The wellbeing of your loved ones may also be uppermost in your mind for now.

20 TUESDAY

Moon Age Day 17 • Moon Sign Cancer

am ....

pm ....

Help comes from all sorts of directions, even if you are not exactly looking for it at the moment. Family members are especially helpful and will be doing all that they can to make your path through life as smooth as they are able. The one thing that is not at all difficult is showing your appreciation.

21 WEDNESDAY

Moon Age Day 18 • Moon Sign Leo

am ....

pm ....

Your pleasure-seeking qualities are much stimulated at present, and you should be embarking on a much more fortunate period when it comes to following your own direction. Much energy is expounded on behalf of family and especially younger people. Socially, there may be a significant upturn if you look out for it..

22 THURSDAY

Moon Age Day 19 • Moon Sign Leo

am ....

pm ....

Emotional rewards are on the way, thanks to the present position of the Sun, which now takes a journey into your solar fourth house. This is a good placement for the Sun around Christmas time, since it puts the emphasis on family life and the many rewards that comes along as a result.

23 FRIDAY
Moon Age Day 20 • Moon Sign Leo

am ....

pm ....

Calm and unhurried in your approach to life generally, you should not be thrown too much off-course by the many needs that others have of you just at present. On the last Friday before Christmas you will want to do all that you can to spread your usual good cheer, though this is something that you are inclined to do most of the time.

24 SATURDAY
Moon Age Day 21 • Moon Sign Virgo

am ....

pm ....

It is clear that family and friends occupy a central place in your thinking today, which is why you will be spending as much time in their company as circumstances allow. You do your best to avoid outsiders, though such is the intensely social quality of your nature that you tend to attract them anyway.

25 SUNDAY
Moon Age Day 22 • Moon Sign Virgo

am ....

pm ....

The festive spirit is boosted tenfold as Christmas Day coincides with your lunar high for the month. This should spell fun and games all round, not to mention the possibility of impromptu gatherings and associations with people who you do not get to see all that often. Make the most of a good day.

← NEGATIVE TREND							POSITIVE TREND →			
-5	-4	-3	-2	-1		+1	+2	+3	+4	+5
				▓	LOVE					
					MONEY	▓	▓			
					LUCK	▓				
					VITALITY	▓	▓			

26 MONDAY
Moon Age Day 23 • Moon Sign Libra

am ....

pm ....

You can be the star attraction when it comes to making a favourable impression on the people in your vicinity. Co-operation is very important in social gatherings, where you should be the life and soul of any party. You can be especially entertaining company to have around, which is why people seek you out.

27 TUESDAY
Moon Age Day 24 • Moon Sign Libra

am ....

pm ....

Social calls come along from people who are close to you, though probably those from outside the family. All the same, things should quieten down a little and there will be some moments to spend in contemplation. Probably a good day for mulling over plans that you have for the future.

28 WEDNESDAY
Moon Age Day 25 • Moon Sign Scorpio

am ....

pm ....

If you are working today, you can expect some of the best Christmas presents to be coming in terms of the attitude of colleagues. Those Librans who are still at home can have a varied and generally interesting day, especially since now social possibilities come along to brighten the atmosphere.

29 THURSDAY
Moon Age Day 26 • Moon Sign Scorpio

am ....

pm ....

Things could cool down a little now, at least allowing you more chance to catch up on yourself after such a hectic interlude. Help comes your way in practical matters and you should also find that even acquaintances are putting themselves out to be accommodating. There may not be much in the way of movement.

30 FRIDAY
Moon Age Day 27 • Moon Sign Sagittarius

am ....

pm ....

Chances are that you will be called upon to help other people through a difficult patch. Such is the natural sympathy that you show to the world that you are often sought out in this way. As usual, it should be fairly easy for you to find the right answers. Personal confidence may not be as strong as usual.

31 SATURDAY
Moon Age Day 28 • Moon Sign Sagittarius

am ....

pm ....

Time is taken up with social possibilities and with confidence boosting exercises of one sort or another. Leave some space for doing whatever takes your fancy, especially since you are likely to be very much in demand later in the day. You should be careful to make resolutions that you can stick to.

← NEGATIVE TREND								POSITIVE TREND →				
-5	-4	-3	-2	-1		LOVE		+1	+2	+3	+4	+5
						MONEY						
						LUCK						
						VITALITY						

RISING SIGNS
for L I B R A

Look along the top to find your date of birth, and down the side for y
hour (or two) if appropriate for Summer Time.

	SEPTEMBER											
	24	25	26	27	28	29	30	1	2	3	4	5	6

MIDNIGHT		
1	LEO	
2		
3		
4	VIRGO	
5		
AM 6		
7	LIBRA	
8		
9		
10	SCORPIO	
11		
MIDDAY 12	SA	
1		
2		
3		
4		
5		
PM 6		
7		
8		
9		
10		
11		
12		

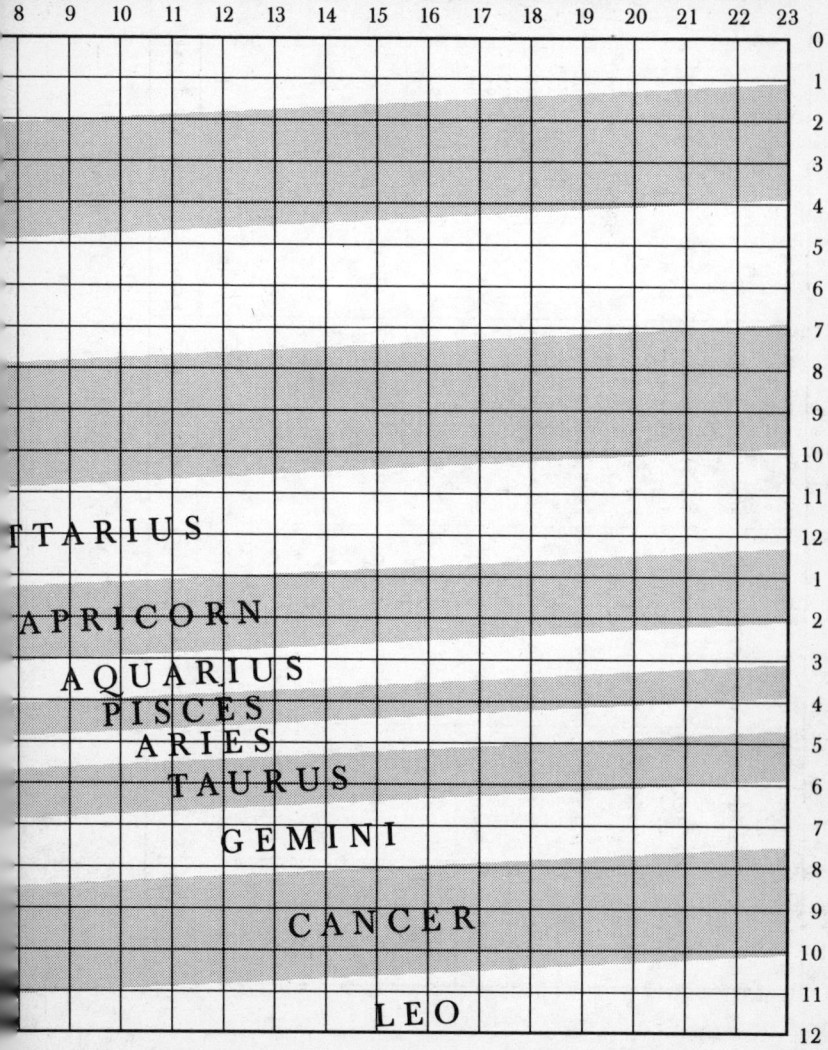

OCTOBER

8	9	10	11	12	13	14	15	16	17	18	19	20	21	22	23

0
1
2
3
4
5
6
7
8
9
10
11

TTARIUS — 12

1

APRICORN — 2

AQUARIUS — 3

PISCES — 4

ARIES — 5

TAURUS — 6

GEMINI — 7

8

CANCER — 9

10

11

LEO — 12

THE ZODIAC AT A GLANCE

Placed	Sign	Symbol	Glyph	Polarity	Element	Quality	Planet	Glyph	Metal	Stone	Opposite
1	Aries	Ram	♈	+	Fire	Cardinal	Mars	♂	Iron	Bloodstone	Libra
2	Taurus	Bull	♉	–	Earth	Fixed	Venus	♀	Copper	Sapphire	Scorpio
3	Gemini	Twins	♊	+	Air	Mutable	Mercury	☿	Mercury	Tiger's Eye	Sagittarius
4	Cancer	Crab	♋	–	Water	Cardinal	Moon	☽	Silver	Pearl	Capricorn
5	Leo	Lion	♌	+	Fire	Fixed	Sun	☉	Gold	Ruby	Aquarius
6	Virgo	Maiden	♍	–	Earth	Mutable	Mercury	☿	Mercury	Sardonyx	Pisces
7	Libra	Scales	♎	+	Air	Cardinal	Venus	♀	Copper	Sapphire	Aries
8	Scorpio	Scorpion	♏	–	Water	Fixed	Pluto	♇	Plutonium	Jasper	Taurus
9	Sagittarius	Archer	♐	+	Fire	Mutable	Jupiter	♃	Tin	Topaz	Gemini
10	Capricorn	Goat	♑	–	Earth	Cardinal	Saturn	♄	Lead	Black Onyx	Cancer
11	Aquarius	Waterbearer	♒	+	Air	Fixed	Uranus	♅	Uranium	Amethyst	Leo
12	Pisces	Fishes	♓	–	Water	Mutable	Neptune	♆	Tin	Moonstone	Virgo

THE ZODIAC, PLANETS
AND CORRESPONDENCES

In the first column of the table of correspondence, I list the signs of the Zodiac as they order themselves around their circle; starting with Aries and finishing with Pisces. In the last column, I list the signs as they will appear as opposites to those in the first column. For example, the sign which will be positioned opposite Aries, in a circular chart will be Libra.

Each sign of the Zodiac is either positive or negative. This by no means suggests that they are either 'good' or 'bad', but that they are either extrovert, outgoing, masculine signs (positive), or introspective, receptive, feminine signs (negative).

Each sign of the Zodiac will belong to one of the four Elements: Fire, Air, Earth or Water. Fire signs are creative and enthusiastic; Air signs are mentally active and thoughtful; Earth signs are constructive and practical; Water signs are emotional and have strong feelings.

Each sign of the Zodiac also belongs to one of the Qualities: Cardinal, Fixed or Mutable. Cardinal signs are initiators and pioneers; Fixed signs are consistent and inflexible; Mutable signs are educators and live to serve.

So, each sign will be either positive or negative, and will belong to one of the Elements and to one of the Qualities. You can see from the table, for example, that Aries is a positive, Cardinal, Fire sign.

The table also shows which planets rule each sign. For example, Mars is the ruling planet of Aries. Each planet represents a particular facet of personality - Mars represents physical energy and drive - and the sign which it rules is the one with which it has most in common,

The table also shows which metals and gem stones are associated with, or correspond with the signs of the Zodiac. Again, the correspondence is made when a metal or stone possesses properties that are held in common with a particular sign of the Zodiac. This system of correspondences can be extended to encompass any group, whether animal, vegetable or mineral - as well as people! For example, each sign of the Zodiac is associated with particular flowers and herbs, with particular animals, with particular towns and countries, and so on.

It is an interesting exercise when learning about astrology, to guess which sign of the Zodiac rules a particular thing, by trying to match its qualities with the appropriate sign.

The News of the Future

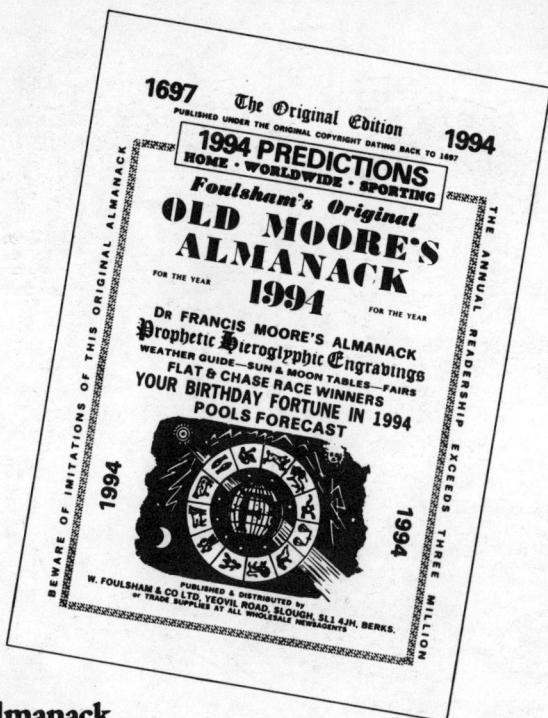

1697 The Original Edition **1994**
PUBLISHED UNDER THE ORIGINAL COPYRIGHT DATING BACK TO 1697

1994 PREDICTIONS
HOME · WORLDWIDE · SPORTING

Foulsham's Original
OLD MOORE'S ALMANACK
FOR THE YEAR **1994** FOR THE YEAR

DR FRANCIS MOORE'S ALMANACK
Prophetic Hieroglyphic Engravings
WEATHER GUIDE—SUN & MOON TABLES—FAIRS
FLAT & CHASE RACE WINNERS
YOUR BIRTHDAY FORTUNE IN 1994
POOLS FORECAST

PUBLISHED & DISTRIBUTED by
W. FOULSHAM & CO LTD, YEOVIL ROAD, SLOUGH, SL1 4JH, BERKS.
or TRADE SUPPLIES AT ALL WHOLESALE NEWSAGENTS.

THE ANNUAL READERSHIP EXCEEDS THREE MILLION

BEWARE OF IMITATIONS OF THIS ORIGINAL ALMANACK

In the Almanack

Racing Tips — All the Classics. Dozens and dozens of lucky dates to follow — for Trainers and Jockeys.

Football and Greyhounds too.

Gardening Guide — Better Everything. Bigger; better; more colour. Whatever you want! Lunar planting is the key.

Fish Attack — Anglers get the upper hand and catch more fish. Dates, times and species to fish are all here.

With Key Zodiac Sign dates of course.

A great New Year investment for you.
An inexpensive, fun gift for your friends.
Look for it at W. H. Smith, John Menzies, Martins and all good newsagents.